RHETORICAL DECEPTION IN THE SHORT FICTION OF HAWTHORNE, POE, AND MELVILLE

Rhetorical Deception in the Short Fiction of Hawthorne, Poe, and Melville

Terry J. Martin

Studies in Comparative Literature
Volume 23

The Edwin Mellen Press
Lewiston•Queenston•Lampeter

Library of Congress Cataloging-in-Publication Data

Martin, Terry J.
  Rhetorical deception in the short fiction of Hawthorne, Poe, and
Melville / Terry J. Martin.
      p.   cm.-- (Studies in comparative literature ; v. 23)
    Includes bibliographical references and index.
    ISBN 0-7734-8240-7 (hc)
      1. Short stories, American--History and criticism. 2. American
fiction--19th century--History and criticism. 3. Hawthorne,
Nathaniel, 1804-1864--Technique. 4. Poe, Edgar Allan, 1809-1849-
-Technique. 5. Melville, Herman, 1819-1891--Technique.
6. Deception in literature. 7. Narration (Rhetoric)   I. Title.
II. Series: Studies in comparative literature (Lewiston, N.Y.) ; v.
23
PS374.S5M38   1998
813' .010903--dc21   98-39987
                                                                                         CIP

This is volume 23 in the continuing series
Studies in Comparative Literature
Volume 23 ISBN 0-7734-8240-7
SCL Series ISBN 0-88946-393-X

A CIP catalog record for this book is available from the British Library.

The Edwin Mellen Press   The Edwin Mellen Press
          Box 450   Box 67
    Lewiston, New York   Queenston, Ontario
    USA 14092-0450   CANADA L0S 1L0

The Edwin Mellen Press, Ltd.
Lampeter, Ceredigion, Wales
UNITED KINGDOM SA48 8LT

Printed in the United States of America

For Toty

Table of Contents

Preface

In his closely reasoned study of a significant rhetorical strategy in the short story fiction of Hawthorne, Melville and Poe, Terry Martin provides a refreshing return to serious and sound analysis in a critical era adrift in foggy generalizations about culture and politics.

Practical criticism, if it is any good at all, inevitably becomes theoretical. And Terry Martin's study is very good indeed. For by carefully analyzing only a few stories by the three major writers of the American romantic period, he helps us understand a generic characteristic of the short story as a form—its frequent tendency to undermine itself, to challenge its surface narrative, and to insist that the reader engage in an essential interpretive activity.

Martin is surely right to attribute this innovative narrative technique largely to the romantic experiment with limited point of view. What Martin terms "ultra deception" is an inevitable implication of the shift away from the old oral teller, whose allegiance was to the received tale, to the single teller/writer who knows only what he sees, and who simultaneously knows that what he sees is not the whole truth. Martin first wisely shows how this technique is not the same as either "trick endings" or traditional satire and then knuckles down to the demanding task of explaining how and why the strategy works.

It is no accident that Poe, an early experimenter with these techniques of concealment and duplicity was also the creator of the convention of the detective story, with its insistence that the reader be involved in the hermeneutic activity of the detective. Martin is right, therefore, to choose "Murders in the Rue Morgue" as one of his examples. He is also right to focus on "Young Goodman Brown" and to show how it is a story that is both allegorical and, at the same time, an undermining of the allegorical tradition on which it depends, a story in which the narrator both accepts and questions the narrative he presents. And, of course, given Martin's central focus, there is no way he could ignore "Benito Cereno," surely the central 19th century document of duplicity.

Terry Martin's concise and compact book is a genuine contribution to the generic study of the short story. Thankfully free of pretentious jargon, clearly and gracefully written, it is a provocative analysis of a central characteristic of the form—one more welcome indication of the new respect with which scholars and critics now consider short fiction.

Charles E. May
California State University at Long Beach

Acknowledgments

No book is ever the work of a single author, despite our cultural obsession with the attribution of authorship as such. I wish to thank the many voices that speak in and through this one. First, I would like to thank the men who comprised my dissertation committee, all of whom provided invaluable advice and encouragement. Chief among these is Joseph Fradin, to whom I owe so much of my appreciation of literature, and whose wisdom, patience, generosity, and good cheer made the writing of this a pleasant task. No less integral to the completion of this book was Neil Schmitz, who greatly enlarged my historical and theoretical awareness, and whose genius continues to illumine my study of American literature. I am likewise indebted to Marcus Klein for his sagacity, critical judgment, and fine sense of humor.

I wish also to acknowledge those who either directly or indirectly helped me with the subsequent revision of this manuscript. Most notable among these are two people who have provided unflagging support, and whose friendship I prize dearly: they are Michael Dolzani, whose vast scholarship has been an inspiration to me, and Janet Joseph, whose excellent stylistic advice has saved many a rough, obscure, or otherwise infelicitous passage of mine from finding its way into print. Special thanks go to Charles E. May, Susan Lohafer, and Wesley T. Mott, who reviewed the manuscript and provided a number of helpful iv

suggestions for revision. I am likewise indebted to my former student assistant Karen Ciha for her painstaking review of much of the secondary criticism of "Benito Cereno," and to the Baldwin-Wallace College English Department Secretary Barb Koeppen for her endless good-natured logistical help.

No less crucial to the process of revision was the institutional support I received from Baldwin-Wallace College. In 1996, I was afforded release time by a Gigax Faculty Development Fund Grant, which was originally endowed by the family of Lester Gigax, longtime friend and trustee of Baldwin-Wallace College.

"Anti-allegory and the Reader in 'Young Goodman Brown,'" which now forms Chapter One, was first published as in Mid-Hudson Language Studies 11 (1988): 31-40. "Detection, Imagination, and the Introduction to 'The Murders in the Rue Morgue,'" which now forms Chapter Two, first appeared in Modern Language Studies 20.4 (1989): 31-45. I am grateful in both cases for permission to reprint.

The jacket design is an original work of art by Alicia L. Maurer, whose talent and fine working manner I greatly appreciate.

Finally, I wish to acknowledge the special love and support of my wife Toty, to whom this book is dedicated, as well as of my parents Don and Myrna Martin and my sister Tris M. Dunn, all of whom have shown great patience and understanding and who have enabled me to follow my joy.

Introduction:

On the Ultra-deceptive Short Story

In the foreword to <u>Studies in Classic American Literature</u>, D. H. Lawrence observes that American authors such as Poe, Hawthorne, and Melville

> refuse everything explicit and always put up a sort of double meaning. They revel in subterfuge. They prefer their truth safely swaddled in an ark of bulrushes, and deposited among the reeds until some friendly Egyptian princess comes to rescue the babe. (viii)

Although Lawrence's criticism of American fiction is often passionately iconoclastic (e.g., Lawrence describes Franklin as a dry and hateful slavedriver and Whitman as "a rather fat old man full of a rather senile, self-conscious sensuosity" [19, 166]), his observation that American fiction is deceptive seems to me to be right on the mark, at least with regard to many of its finest Nineteenth-Century practitioners. To be sure, Lawrence is not the first to make this pronouncement. In "Hawthorne and His Mosses," Melville had over seventy years earlier noted the same quality in Hawthorne's fiction, and his own attempts to disguise his meaning in such works as <u>Pierre</u> have been well documented by Hershel Parker and Leon Howard. Likewise, Poe's work has recently been analyzed from a similar perspective, such as in David Ketterer's fine book, <u>Poe and the Rationale of Deception</u> (1979). Today the idea that classic American fiction is deceptive needs no defense; it has simply become a critical commonplace.

Yet such commonplaces mask as much as they reveal. Deception in literature takes many different forms, and it can have many different purposes. Of course, in a fundamental sense all authors deceive; every narrative, no matter how purportedly true or faithful, distorts experience in some manner, for language necessarily imposes on the flux of experience an arbitrary structure. The problem is simply compounded in the case of fictional narrative, which is by definition something feigned and invented and hence inherently deceptive. Nevertheless, what I propose to examine here is not a quality that all fiction shares. Rather, it is a deliberate and sophisticated rhetorical strategy best exemplified by some of Hawthorne's, Poe's, and Melville's finest short stories, including, respectively, "Young Goodman Brown" (1837; hereafter cited as "YGB"), "The Murders in the Rue Morgue" (1841; hereafter cited as "MRM"), and "Benito Cereno" (1856; hereafter cited as "BC").[1]

Of course, the term rhetorical can be equally ambiguous. In fact, in the pejorative sense rhetoric itself denotes conscious deception of a sort, which can range from an artificial and affected eloquence to the dishonest inflation or masking of the truth. Here, however, I employ it in its traditionally broad sense as the art of persuasion, the means by which authors aim to move their audience, whether their intention is to convince intellectually, sway emotionally, satisfy esthetically, or achieve any combination thereof. Unfortunately, the term contains an additional ambiguity as it relates to fiction. In The Rhetoric of Fiction, Wayne Booth distinguishes between "the rhetoric in fiction, as overt and recognizable appeal (the most extreme form being authorial commentary), and fiction as rhetoric in the larger sense, an aspect of the whole work viewed as a total act of

---

[1] "Benito Cereno" is, of course, generally referred to as a novella rather than as a short story. Nevertheless, I include it in the category of short story advisedly, since it is often included in short-story anthologies, and I find that it meets the criteria most short-story theorists point to for inclusion in the genre: that is, it has economy, unity of effect, and brevity (it meets, for example, Poe's criterion of being able to be read at one sitting, E. M. Forster's of being less than 50,000 words [5-6], and Austin Wright's of "[not being] much longer than 'Heart of Darkness'" [50], etc.).

communication" (415). I will be employing the term in the former sense, since I will be concerned with a rhetorical strategy that is not a dimension of all fiction but is instead unique to certain stories. My one reservation with Booth's definition is that in the specific stories I discuss, the authorial appeal, though recognizable, is covert rather than overt. Such a use of the term is, however, consistent with Booth's, who devotes much of his analysis to the "disguised rhetoric of modern fiction" (xiii; my emphasis), of which the stories I analyze here are significant precursors.

The rhetorical strategy I will examine here represents a milestone in the development of fictional technique. Indeed, it fundamentally prefigures Henry James's celebrated use of distorting "centers of consciousness," and especially of his ultra-unreliable narrators such as the Governess of "The Turn of the Screw" and Jeffrey Aspern of "The Aspern Papers." In many ways, it also anticipates the metafictional techniques of such writers as Vladimir Nabokov, John Barth, and Alain Robbe-Grillet. What is innovative about "YGB," "MRM," and "BC" is that the reader is not only guilefully misled through a sophisticated use of the limited point of view but never expressly apprised of the deception. This rhetorical strategy represents a radical departure from convention, for, as Wayne Booth points out, pre-Jamesian readers' "habitual experience of narrative testimony led them to expect reliability unless unreliability were clearly proved" (Fiction, 366-67). Moreover, the stories are structured as tests, for each of them poses a problem that is at once epistemological and moral. That is, the point of view that the reader is tricked or seduced into adopting is self-deluded, and the viewpoint character himself, implicated in crime. The stories specifically challenge the reader to transcend the delusion and to interpret correctly. The stories are thereby significant as a group because of 1) their highly sophisticated and unprecedented use of deception, 2) the quantum leap in the kind of active reader that each implies, 3) the fact that their common rhetorical strategy first appears exclusively in short fiction of the American Renaissance, and 4) the dependence of their rhetorical strategy on the enabling conditions and unique suitability of the short story form.

Of course, these stories share many elements in common with earlier related works. Like all great artists, Hawthorne, Poe, and Melville borrow heavily from tradition. However, these writers display an astonishing originality in terms of the new and sophisticated uses to which they put received forms. To appreciate what is innovative about these stories requires seeing them as a total pattern of communication in contrast to those of other related prose forms that employ deception. In the pages that follow, I will try to give a clearer sense of what distinguishes these stories as a group. For the sake of convenience, I will refer to them as ultra-deceptive short narratives, for they employ a far greater degree of deception than other narratives of their day, and I believe that their challenge to the reader to discover and transcend the deception is the main point of the story.

The ultra-deceptive short story and the common ironic or trick ending

The kind of deception employed here by Hawthorne, Poe, and Melville differs substantially from the technique of the surprise ending (or trick ending or final twist), which was the trademark of such masters as Guy de Maupassant and O. Henry. Of course, both sets of authors purposefully mislead their readers, but de Maupassant and O. Henry only do so for a limited duration. Their stories are structured in such a way that what they cleverly conceal throughout gains the greatest possible dramatic effect by its sudden revelation at the end. For instance, the narrator of Maupassant's classic story "The Necklace" waits until the very last line to announce that the necklace is false—thus ironically negating the ten years of hard work, self-sacrifice, and ruinous debt undertaken by Monsieur and Madame Loisel to replace it after it is lent to them and lost at a ball. In fact, not only does the narrator withhold information, but he deliberately seeks to produce the opposite impression throughout the tale both by dramatizing Monsieur and Madame Loisel's conviction that the necklace is genuine and by portraying its owner as a lady of wealth and rank who would presumably not use fake jewelry. Likewise, to cite just one example from O. Henry's vast repertoire of trick endings, the narrator of "A Cosmopolite in a Café" chooses to wait until the final line to reveal E. Rushmore Coglan's fiercely patriotic attachment to his native town, Mattawamkeag, Maine, despite having given every indication throughout the story that Coglan rejects all forms of regional chauvinism (13). In both cases the deferral of crucial information is rhetorically designed to increase the reader's surprise and aesthetic pleasure in the final ironic reversal. The deception thus proves temporary and provisional; at the proper moment, the secret is explicitly revealed, enabling the reader to achieve full understanding. I will be concerned, however, with a kind of deception which is never explicitly revealed, or which is, in Melville's phrase, "not obtruded upon everyone alike" (Piazza, 245), and which thus differs in its design, scope, effect, and implications.

The ultra-deceptive short story and satire

The strategy of deception employed by Hawthorne, Poe, and Melville likewise resembles certain earlier works of satire, yet nevertheless differs from them in at least two important respects. Satire shares a common ironic structure and, in some forms, a refusal to express its meaning literally or explicitly. To take two justly famed examples, neither Defoe in "The Shortest Way with Dissenters" nor Swift in "A Modest Proposal" ever expressly states that his work is satirical. Both rely instead on the reader's perception of ironic intent in order to communicate their ideas. Moreover, both Defoe and Swift begin their satires by luring us into the same kind of trap that the later American authors employ: they create credible narrative voices which the reader will be persuaded to accept, at least initially, as genuine. Thus, their respective narrators are educated and appear to argue rationally, and there is no early sign of the vast discrepancy between their stated views and the implied authors' own, or, for that matter, between the views stated in the essays and those that the majority of readers might be expected to

6

entertain (such as the belief that raising children to be eaten is shocking and barbaric, or that killing people for disagreeing is decidedly un-Christian). It is only gradually that such discrepancies become apparent, and thus part of the fun is to see how long the author can keep the reader going before the irony becomes too evident. Furthermore, Defoe and Swift require that readers recognize the moral absurdity of their speakers' views and consciously reject them with laughter. It is not a question of ambiguity; to fail to reject the speakers' views is quite simply to miss the whole point. That is the risk of the kind of irony that Booth has termed "stable irony" (Irony, 1), and Defoe's satire was, in fact, widely mistaken for a legitimate and persuasive plea for the use of terrorism against dissenters.[2] This same risk is to a certain extent taken by Hawthorne, Poe, and Melville, whose stories also have, as a result, been frequently misunderstood.

Nevertheless, the two sets of works differ in significant ways. First of all, satire depends for its effect upon the shared laughter of author and reader, without which it loses its unique power of persuasion. Hence, any satire that leaves readers in doubt about the attitude they are expected to assume toward the subject matter may to that extent be said to have failed. However, in all three of the stories by Hawthorne, Poe, and Melville, the reader lacks the certainty of ironic intent for which laughter so often provides the cue. The stories may contain occasional comic material, but they do not ultimately provoke a comic response from their audience. Instead, two of the works, "YGB" and "BC," end in a remarkably gloomy manner. Brown's strangely disconcerting failure to find peace and to resolve his doubts and Benito Cereno's eerily troubled death elicit serious reflection rather than laughter. "MRM" concludes with a series of odd ironic boasts by Dupin which I have never heard anyone describe as humorous. The irony is, in fact, so subtle that it may require several readings even to detect,

---

[2] Defoe was eventually forced to explain that the piece was satirical in another pamphlet entitled A Brief Explanation of a Late Pamphlet, entituled [sic], The Shortest Way with the Dissenters. See Sutherland 43-48.

since it follows what appears so plainly to be a tour de force of ratiocination. Instead of finding the generally clear intention of satire, many first-time readers of these stories (especially of "YGB" and "BC") have reported to me that they feel confused.

That confusion stems from a further difference between satire and the aforementioned stories by Hawthorne, Poe, and Melville, which is the greater symbolic and epistemological complexity of the latter. Of course, these stories are to a certain extent typical of the modern short story in general, which is notable for its often complex and confusing nature. According to seminal short-story theorist Mary Rohrberger,

> The short story . . . leaves the reader with a set of emotions that cannot be easily sorted; he is often confused as to meaning, and he finds it almost impossible to state the theme in a sentence or two; his satisfaction must be postponed until he has answered the questions presented to him by means of the symbolic structure of the story. (106-7)

Thus, one cannot hope to understand a narrative such as "BC" without puzzling out the relation between the events in the story and the complex symbolism of, say, the heraldic device on the San Dominick's stern-piece, in which appears "a dark satyr in a mask, holding his foot on the prostrate neck of a writhing figure, likewise masked" (49). Since this emblem functions as an archetype of political power within the world of "Benito Cereno," it significantly undermines Delano's repeated claims to legitimacy and benevolence in his role as captain, as does the symbolic greyness and duplicity depicted in the natural world. All such symbols must, of course, be brought as far as possible into a unified comprehension of the story. The stories thus raise questions that need to be puzzled out before full understanding is achieved, questions which could not be permitted in satire without diluting or negating the main point.

The ultra-deceptive short story and the use of the limited point of view in narrative fiction

In a certain sense, deception is by definition built into the very structure of the limited point of view. Unable to grasp things in their totality, a finite fictional subject is doomed to errors in perception or in judgment, as is the reader who takes such perception for unequivocal truth. However, narratives told from a limited point of view do not necessarily aim at deceiving their readers, nor are their readers inevitably without authorial aid of some kind in measuring the deception. Of course, twentieth-century readers have the advantage here, for, trained as much by Henry James as by Freudian psychoanalysis, they take unreliability for granted, whether in a narrator or fictional subject. Pre-Twentieth-Century readers were far more dependent on direct authorial aid in recognizing unreliability. As the astute historian Henry Adams once observed of the premodern age,

> Psychological study was still simple. . . . Henry James had not yet taught the world to read a volume for the pleasure of seeing the lights of his burning-glass turned on alternate sides of the same figure. (163)

Determining the relative difficulty that the limited point of view presents to the reader therefore depends both on the context of the expectations of the reading public—which in pre-Civil War America was, by modern standards, relatively naïve—and on the rhetorical application to which such a narrative technique is put. Before Hawthorne, Poe, and Melville, no one had so fully exploited the potential for rhetorical deception in the limited point of view.

Consider, for example, two earlier works that make use of the limited point of view: Oliver Goldsmith's The Vicar of Wakefield (1766), written in the first-person, and Jane Austen's Emma (1816), written in the third-person. Like their counterparts in the ultra-deceptive stories, the protagonists of both The Vicar of Wakefield and Emma are occasionally deluded. In the former, Dr. Primrose is fooled by the announcement of Olivia's death, misconstrues the motives of Sir

William Thornhill alias Mr. Burchell, and occasionally gives vent to a most unbecoming and wrong-headed despair. In Emma, Emma entertains perhaps well-intended but seriously misguided plans for Harriet Smith, and variously misreads the nature of Mr. Elton's, Frank Churchill's, Harriet Smith's, and even Mr. Knightley's affections. Nonetheless, in early works of this type such deceptions are almost always temporary—that is, they are almost invariably exposed and resolved in the course of the narrative. Often, too, there is overt authorial aid to the reader in recognizing them while they are occurring. The introduction to Emma, for instance, alerts us openly to Emma's defects:

> The real evils of Emma's situation were the power of having rather too much her own way, and a disposition to think a little too well of herself; these were the disadvantages which threatened alloy to her many enjoyments. The danger, however, was at present so unperceived, that they did not by any means rank as misfortunes with her. (Austen 1)

The author may also communicate such information via another character's advice or warning that serves simultaneously to indicate to the reader the real state of affairs. Such a role is played in The Vicar of Wakefield by Sir William Thornhill/Mr. Burchell, who exposes the true nature of the villains, and in Emma by Mr. Knightley, who frankly criticizes Emma's faults. Finally, the protagonists of both works are ultimately undeceived and thereby serve to correct the reader's understanding. Thus, although the limited point of view may in this case present momentary difficulties, it finally provides no major obstacle to—or lasting test of—the reader's understanding

By contrast, the ultra-deceptive short story far more self-consciously employs deception to test its readers. In fact, in all three stories, the authors explicitly challenge the reader to match wits with the protagonist and to interpret correctly. The very presence of such an unusual feature in these stories in itself suggests how elusive these authors understood their meaning to be. In "BC," the narrator issues this challenge at the outset:

> Captain Delano's surprise might have deepened into some

uneasiness had he not been a person of a singularly undistrustful good nature, not liable, except on extraordinary and repeated incentives, and hardly then, to indulge in personal alarms, any way involving the imputation of malign evil in man. Whether, in view of what humanity is capable, such a trait implies, along with a benevolent heart, more than ordinary quickness and accuracy of intellectual perception, may be left to the wise to determine. (47)

The question calls for a critical appraisal of Delano, and it is underscored by Melville's refusal to pronounce a ready verdict for the reader. (That is to say, there are in reality two questions in this passage: first, whether or not Delano is intellectually quick and accurate—a question that is answered by default, for Delano clearly fails, despite repeated clues, to discover the plot against him and his ship until fate forces Babo to reveal it; and second, whether or not Delano has a benevolent heart. It is the latter and more significant question that Melville never explicitly answers; indeed, the question itself is often missed entirely by readers, since it almost seems to be syntactically sandwiched into the sentence as a given.) Delano regards evil as entirely external to himself, yet the deeper thrust of Melville's challenge is to consider the possibility that "good captain" Delano (47)—and, by extension, the country that he represents—is evil.

"MRM" likewise contains a challenge in its elaborate introduction. Poe prepares the reader for the narrative proper by describing the ideal player/analyst/reader, whose interpretive skills the reader is by implication exhorted to display (or to develop). In addition, Poe establishes a hierarchy of qualitatively different modes of reading when he defines true analysis to be an act of imagination: "The truly imaginative," he declares, is "never otherwise than analytic" (4: 150). Poe thereby implicitly challenges the reader to exercise true imagination in interpretation. Finally, "YGB" also challenges the reader to ascertain the true state of affairs by asking, "Had Goodman Brown fallen asleep in the forest, and only dreamed a wild dream of a witch-meeting?" (10: 89). The question thrusts the reader into the role of literary detective, who must now hunt for evidence and determine which construction (dream or reality) is the truest or most likely, as well as what the story means in light of either. If the narrator's subsequent comment, "Be it so, if you will" (10: 89), seems to leave the decision entirely up to the reader, the choices are actually carefully restricted by the narrative context, which the careful reader will wish to consult anew. It should be noted that each of these challenges posits a far more active, even aggressive, implied reader than fiction had heretofore known.

The ultra-deceptive stories are also distinguished as a group by their innovative sense of gamesmanship. For instance, all three contain mysteries to be solved (in "YGB," what exactly happens to Brown in the woods; in "MRM," who killed the L'Espanayes; and in "BC," what the actual state of affairs is on board the San Dominick). "MRM" even begins with an extensive discussion of games and of playing strategy. Poe stacks the narrative with disguised clues and double entendres, creating, in effect, a linguistic game in which the purpose of reading becomes the discovery of what is concealed. Melville and Hawthorne encode similar puzzles in their work. "Undo it, cut it, quick" (76) blurts a wizened old sailor in "BC" as he tosses an intricate knot at Captain Delano. The knot, of course, symbolizes a test for the intellect, and readers may well make the connection between the knot in Delano's hand and the one in his head (not to mention the one in their own in struggling to unravel the complexity of the narrative). The object of the game is thus to unravel the knot before Delano, as well as to avoid passively reproducing his errors. Like Poe, Melville incorporates numerous disguised clues which turn the act of reading itself into a detective game. Although "YGB" makes no explicit allusion to games, such a quality is nevertheless implicit in its very structure in the form of its teasing tone, the ironic play of its language, and the interpretive struggle which, like the others, it fosters between the reader and the protagonist.

Finally, the ultra-deceptive stories of Hawthorne, Poe, and Melville are startlingly modern in their active and self-conscious engagement with hermeneutic questions. By structuring themselves as a series of unstable signs or clues, they are texts that not only call attention to the need for interpretation but are also <u>about</u> the process of interpretation itself. Indeed, each work metafictionally portrays characters (mis)interpreting events to examine how interpretation may be distorted by the structures of understanding that characters—and, by extension, readers—bring to it. In all three stories, the protagonist functions as an avatar of failed interpretation, and the delusions that each undergoes are symbolically shown to be endemic to his very system of understanding itself. These stories thus entail a more fundamental critique of the observing consciousness than in previous literary uses of the limited point of view, where the protagonist's mistakes are often presented more sympathetically as the result of temporary lapses in judgment (as in <u>The Vicar of Wakefield</u>) or of inexperience regarding the public effects of private designs (as in <u>Emma</u>), or some such other cause. Thus, Dr. Primrose is never actually deluded in his faith that honesty and virtue are (at least within the world of Goldsmith's novel) rewarded in this life. Likewise, Emma, who consistently misreads the intentions of people around her, is not wrong in her fundamental conviction that (again, within the world of Austen's novel) people should only marry their social equals and that marrying well and caring for her father are, after all, her valid aims in life. Moreover, in both novels, a happy ending eventually confirms the world-view of each respective protagonist: Dr. Primrose's family emerges from ignominy and is restored to wealth and respectability. In addition, his son George is reunited with Arabella, his daughter Sophia marries Sir William Thornhill, and even his daughter Olivia is saved from shame when she learns that her supposedly fraudulent marriage to Squire Thornhill is actually valid. Likewise, Emma not only ends up happily married to the right man, but also finds her protégée and rival Harriet Smith safely removed to her proper social sphere. However, the delusions suffered by the protagonists of the ultra-deceptive stories are not merely local or temporary, but rather sweeping or overriding, and they are thus indicative of a blindness at the very center of their understanding. In fact, in each of the three stories I will analyze, a radical critique of a major world view is implied: "YGB" exposes the flaws of New England Puritanism; "BC," those of a kind of pragmatic Yankee idealism, and "MRM," those of Nineteenth-Century logical positivism.

The ultra-deceptive short story and the modern short story

As stated earlier, the ultra-deceptive story shares certain features in common with the modern short story, including the complex and (at least initially) perplexing relationship between the story's literal sense and its underlying symbolic structure. However, the ultra-deceptive story is an exceptional instance of the modern short story and is distinguished from it by a specific congruence of features. The difference is best noted by contrast to what Rohrberger defines as the prototypical modern short story, Hawthorne's "My Kinsman, Major Molineux." Like "YGB," "My Kinsman" presents a defamiliarized landscape and masterfully employs the limited point of view to heighten the reader's sense of puzzlement at the odd and contrary events to which its protagonist Robin is continually exposed. Nevertheless, Hawthorne tips his hand at the end of the tale. Robin does not remain deluded: he learns to laugh at himself, he abandons his childish expectations of having his way made for him, he learns to speak with adult irony, and he comes to accept his own complicity in his kinsman's humiliation. Robin attains, in other words, wisdom of a sort, which, if not altogether comforting, is nevertheless necessary to his growth and maturation as a human being. To that extent Robin serves to guide the reader's response, who is similarly able to achieve understanding not only of what it means for a boy to come of age, but also—since Robin's self-discovery is inadvertently accompanied by the discovery of a social conspiracy—of how sordid and cruel were the origins of the American revolution. The ultra-deceptive story refuses to offer such overt aids to understanding. Brown's lifelong gloom and despair do not provide a positive model of reader response, nor do they in any way exemplify the view of the implied author. Even in those cases when the conclusion of an ultra-deceptive story seems to offer an exemplary explanation of mysterious events (such as Dupin's solving the crime, or the scales dropping away from Delano's eyes), the explanation is itself misleading. Hence, as its name suggests, the ultra-deceptive story employs additional obstacles to understanding, and it is structured more like a test than the modern short story in general.

The ultra-deceptive short story and the "second story"

Of all extant categories of stories, the ultra-deceptive short story most resembles what Armine Kotin Mortimer has called "second stories." The former might in fact be said to be a member of the latter, although so restricted and specialized a form as to constitute a distinct class. Still, the apparent similarities are notable. Both entail the discovery of a story that is not explicitly stated as such. Indeed, Mortimer's definition of second stories might at first glance seem to apply wholesale to the ultra-deceptive story:

> [T]he action of these [i.e., of second] stories on the reader is such that the reader is actively solicited to recognize that undercurrent, encoded in different ways, and in so doing to create a second story that is not told outright. (276)

Moreover, just as in the case of the ultra-deceptive story, several of Mortimer's examples involve the rhetorical use of a "defective . . . limited vision" (291). Finally, Mortimer observes, "In the most frustrating examples, [the second story] never comes to light, though it leaves clues" (276), and she adds, "to bring [the second story] to light . . . is to adopt the role of the detective" (290). Nevertheless, there are significant differences between the two kinds of stories. Mortimer's is a broad category that includes all stories that contain second stories, even when those second stories follow from "obvious" implications (281). The ultra-deceptive story, it will be recalled, is anything but obvious. Moreover, Mortimer describes stories that complement the explicit or surface-level narrative, whereas in the case of the ultra-deceptive story, the underlying story inverts or negates it.

Thus, Mortimer emphasizes that surface-level incidents in second stories are "not red herrings" (294), whereas they perforce constitute red-herrings in the ultra-deceptive story. I am nevertheless indebted to Mortimer for her lively and suggestive analysis.

A rhetorical study such as the present one can significantly contribute to an understanding of the historical development of the implied reader in Western fiction. As short story defenders point out, historians and theorists of prose fiction generally focus on the novel, which is often regarded as synonymous with prose fiction (May 131-32). For instance, Wolfgang Iser's groundbreaking study The Implied Reader: Patterns of Communication in Prose Fiction from Bunyan to Beckett focuses exclusively on the novel and thereby ignores the special contribution of the short story to the development of the implied reader. Iser is concerned with marking the shift from passive to active reading, or from overt authorial aid and intrusion to the so-called disappearance of the author, who, in James Joyce's celebrated phrase, "like the God of the creation, remains within or behind or beyond or above his handiwork, invisible, refined out of existence, indifferent, paring his fingernails" (215). For Iser, the critical transition occurs with the rise of the realistic novel. He writes, "The stages of transition are clearly discernible in the nineteenth century, and one of them is virtually a half-way point in the development: the so-called realistic novel" (102). However, it is possible to trace alternate lines of development that at once complement and complicate Iser's model. Certainly, short fiction has made its own unique demands on readers, and an examination of those demands, especially in exceptionally complicated and challenging exemplars, will reveal nuances in the implied reader that an exclusive concern with novels is bound to overlook.

Indeed, the short story as a form lends itself to certain uses to which the novel, by virtue of its greater length and bagginess, is restricted. Thus, it is no coincidence that the rhetorical strategy that I examine here appears in conjunction with the rise of the short story, for the unity and focus of the short-story form were best able to produce it. It is simply much more difficult to sustain over several hundred pages the persuasive masking of a deluded point of view, especially when the challenge of unmasking it forms the implicit point of the narrative. (Certain novels such as Dom Casmurro by Machado de Assis are perhaps notable exceptions to this rule, but the stories I discuss here significantly predate them.) In addition, the novel almost invariably gives rise to other competing interests and hence to an overall diffusion of focus that would tend to inhibit the strategy discussed here. It is, for instance, difficult to imagine Moby Dick told from the sole point of view of (at least partly) deluded Ahab. So much of the extraordinary richness and detail of the narrative would inevitably be suppressed by Ahab's monomaniacal focus. By the same token, the novelist who seeks to render the rhetorical strategy of the ultra-deceptive story in novelistic form may end up sacrificing one of the greatest strengths of that form, which is its sheer breadth and inclusiveness.

I hope the present study will also shed light on three of the greatest short-story masterpieces in literature, as well as on the artistic designs and techniques of Hawthorne, Poe, and Melville. Other candidates for ultra-deceptive status might be advanced, such as Hawthorne's "Roger Malvin's Burial," Poe's "Ligeia," or Melville's "Bartleby the Scrivener." I chose not to include these particular stories because, although each is told by a first-person deluded narrator (or from the limited point of view of a deluded protagonist) and displays the requisite authorial refusal to clarify, two of the stories end on an extraordinarily ambiguous note: it is difficult to determine whether Reuben Bourne's final repentance in "Roger Malvin's Burial" represents the end of his delusion or merely a more mystified continuation of it; likewise, the narrator of "Bartleby the Scrivener" has been variously interpreted as experiencing a final change of heart towards Bartleby and as remaining just as firmly entrenched in his delusive Wall Street Values. As for the narrator of "Ligeia," his self-proclaimed opium addiction, lack of memory, and madness are so prominent as almost to discredit beforehand his testimony of Ligeia's resurrection. In any event, if others find the coined category of ultra-deceptive short stories meaningful, I will be happy to listen to any case made for admitting other candidates to this literary subgenre.

Chapter One

Anti-allegory and the Reader in "Young Goodman Brown"

Although "Young Goodman Brown" (hereafter "YGB") has been read as a straight allegory by at least one critic and its allegorical features noted by many, none, to my knowledge, has seen allegory itself to be a subject of Hawthorne's artistic examination in this perennially fascinating tale. I believe, though, that form and theme are more closely joined than has hitherto been noted, and that "YGB" is a parable about the failure of allegory as a cognitive system of understanding. In this chapter, I will be especially interested in the way in which the story rhetorically enacts this failure in the experience of the reader.

Whether or not "YGB" is read as a straight allegory, no one will deny that it is full of allegorical features. Hawthorne even goes out of his way to emphasize them, nudging the reader in the very second sentence that Faith was "aptly named" (10: 74), as if such a possibility were not immediately evident. Other allegorical features in the story include Goodman Brown's Everyman-like name, the dreamlike nature of the plot, the generic guide and journey, the frequent emphasis on the pink ribbons, the lack of mimetic naturalness, the employment of obvious antithetical contrasts such as good/evil, town/forest, day/night, and so on. All such features collectively alert the reader of the tale's genre.

The identification of genre is important because it also signals a corresponding attitude or expectation, hence a mode of reading, in the reader. As
Alastair Fowler argues in <u>Kinds of Literature: An Introduction to the Theory of
Genres and Modes</u>, "The generic markers that cluster at the beginning of a work
have a strategic role in guiding the reader. They help to establish, as soon as
possible, an appropriate mental 'set' that allows the work's generic codes to be
read" (88). To suggest all of those expectations, both conscious and unconscious,
would be impossible; nonetheless, certain basic expectations invariably accrue
upon even a limited acquaintance with the genre, and Hawthorne could count on
his readers' familiarity with the conventions of such a widely read work as
Bunyan's <u>Pilgrim's Progress</u>. Thus, in an allegory, Hawthorne's audience would
naturally expect to see characters who personify abstract qualities. They would
expect the action to develop within the context of a dualistic, antithetical, and
generally theological scheme of values. They would expect a precedence of the
moral, political or historical meaning over the literal meaning. And perhaps most
importantly, they would expect a clear didactic intention (cf. the definitions of
allegory in <u>The Concise Oxford Dictionary of Literary Terms</u> and <u>A Dictionary of
Modern Critical Terms</u>.)

However, "YGB" baffles these expectations. For one thing, the ending of
the story is disconcerting; its meaning, uncertain. One critic writing in 1876
called "YGB" a "terrible and lurid parable" with a horrifying "revelation of evil"
(Lathrop 203). Another in 1906 observed that "the effect [of 'YGB'] is decidedly
unpleasant" (Stearns 181). A later biographer mentioned the story's "unrelieved
gloom" (Stewart 69). As distinguished a critic as Henry James felt compelled to
dismiss "YGB" precisely because of this problem; it was a "picture," he claimed,
and not a "parable," because "if it meant anything it would mean too much" (99).
The story lacks the clear resolution and obvious poetic justice that one finds in
"The Man of Adamant," in which the reader is well prepared for the protagonist's
final metamorphosis into stone (11: 168-69). In "YGB," the conclusion raises

more questions than it answers, and it leaves most readers with a vague uneasiness.

That uneasiness stems in part from Hawthorne's elusive purpose, the difficulty of perceiving which has been well documented by Harold F. Mosher, Jr. After all, in allegory readers are accustomed to a self-evident didactic intention. As Edward A. Bloom notes, "Obscurity . . . has never been considered an attribute of allegory. . . . Under neoclassical formalism allegory came to be judged as a vehicle not only of morality, but of clarity and rationality as well" (174, 178). In Allegory: The Theory of a Symbolic Mode, Angus Fletcher confirms, "Allegorical intention is in general a simple matter" (323). Nevertheless, "YGB" distinctly challenges the interpreter. A typical response to the story is that of Stearns, who wonders, "Whatever may have been Hawthorne's design[?]" (181). If the strength of the subsequent critical debate serves as any indication, the confusion remains widespread. I believe that the key to this confusion lies in the story's subtle negation of the very norms that it evokes.

Perhaps the best example of the story's subversion of the allegorical norm is the narrator's direct question to the reader, "Had Goodman Brown fallen asleep in the forest and only dreamed a wild dream of a witch-meeting? . . . Be it so, if you will" (10: 89). Simply put, the question is impermissible in allegory because it violates authorial control, which many theorists point to as the definitive characteristic of the genre (Bloom 164; Fletcher 304-5). The question seems, that is, to concede freedom of choice to the reader in a context in which the reader is never free. According to Fletcher, the reader of allegory "is not allowed to take up any attitude he chooses, but is told by the author's devices of intentional control just how he shall interpret what is before him" (323). By apparently throwing open the story to multiple interpretations, the narrator's question unsettles what the genre itself seeks to fix.

More importantly, the narrator's question undermines the ideal meaning— the sine qua non of allegory—by introducing an epistemological dilemma. In allegory, the ideal meaning, or tenor, is granted priority over the literal meaning both by literary convention and the simple working principle that the latter is intended as a vehicle to convey the former. Indeed, to Dante the literal meaning of any figure was entirely negligible; it was a mere "vesture" which the writer could be expected to strip off, if asked, in order to "show the true sense" (qtd. in Lewis 48). Coleridge's definition of allegory supports this view: as Fletcher sums it up, "In allegory there is always an attempt to categorize logical orders first, and fit them to convenient phenomena second, to set forth ideal systems first, and illustrate them second" (18). The priority of the ideal meaning requires the suppression of the literal or empirical truth of the vehicle. As Fletcher explains, "Allegory does not accept the world of experience and the senses; it thrives on their overthrow, replacing them with ideas" (323). For instance, most readers would not presume to impeach the truth of Bunyan's Pilgrim's Progress because it takes the form of a dream vision. Bunyan expects his readers to ignore the notoriously equivocal and unstable form of his vehicle (i.e., a dream) in favor of the absolute and stable ideal truth that it is supposed to represent, which is the Protestant view of salvation. However, in "YGB," the narrator's question undermines the ideal meaning by calling attention to the status of the vehicle and thereby asserting a rival truth-claim for the world of experience. In fact, the question even inverts the relationship between tenor and vehicle, implying the primacy of actuality over the ideal content of what is "only . . . a dream" (my emphasis). Thus, the reader is no longer authorized to decode the ideal meaning until he or she first determines the exact empirical status of Brown's experience (i.e., dream or reality). The focus epistemologically shifts, in other words, from what Brown ideally sees to how—or even whether—he sees it, which means that the allegorical interpreter must first become a literary detective to see whether an allegorical meaning is even justified.

The allegorical norm is further subverted by the narrator's detached, ironic point of view. As D. M. McKeithan was the first to indicate, Brown is a highly unreliable character (95). Using a variety of rhetorical techniques, the narrator systematically calls into question both Brown's judgment and perception.[1] Perhaps the most prominent means is the portrayal of Brown as a naive and credulous simpleton who judges hastily and on ill-founded, flimsy evidence. His idealizing tendency has been widely noted. In addition, Hawthorne applies the most equivocal language to Brown's sensory perception. In the woods, things "seem to" (10: 82, 83), "perhaps" (10: 79), and "almost" (10: 76) happen, which is different than saying that they actually do occur. Moreover, the narrator prefaces every identification with such obscure, indecisive terms as "shape" (10: 86), "form" (10: 86, 87) and "figure" (10: 78, 81, 86, 87), as if to underscore the mediating and equivocal power of appearances. By the time Brown identifies his mother and father in wreaths of smoke, the very evanescence of the medium belies him. Contrarily, sense impressions in daylight or in the town are never couched in uncertain language.

Another means of undermining Brown's judgment is conflicting sensory data, in which Hawthorne employs the evidence of one sense to repudiate or discredit the impression of another. When, for example, Brown hears the approaching voices of the minister and Deacon Gookin, he is unable to confirm their presence visually, despite his alert vigilance: "Brown alternately crouched and stood on tiptoe, pulling aside the branches and thrusting forth his head as far as he durst without discerning so much as a shadow. . . . [I]t could not be seen that they intercepted, even for a moment, the faint gleam from the strip of bright sky, athwart which they must have passed" (10: 81). Of course, this failure to corroborate the evidence of one sense by that of another in no way deters Brown from his conviction that the voices are authentic. Likewise, Brown's conviction that the staff given by the devil to Goody Cloyse turns into a writhing serpent on

---

[1] Particularly good discussions of Brown's epistemological failures include those by David Levin, Paul J. Hurley, Michael J. Colacurcio, Sheldon W. Liebman, Norman H. Hostetler, and Terence Martin (not to be confused with the present writer). I have tried to add to their findings here.

the ground is discredited by the fact that he never actually sees it. He "could not take cognizance . . . [o]f this fact" (10: 79), for at the critical moment "[h]e had cast up his eyes in astonishment" (10: 79), and, by the time he lowers them, both Goody and the staff are gone.

Hawthorne also undermines Brown's judgment by means of the latter's manifest reliance on appearances. Hawthorne suggests the precarious nature of Brown's faith in such scenes as that of the falling ribbon (10: 83). However, the preceding scene prepares the reader for it. When Brown, with a "heavy sickness of his heart," momentarily doubts heaven, he looks up to the sky for reassurance: "Yet there was the blue arch, and the stars brightening in it" (10: 82). The irony should be clear to any critical reader: one does not confirm the existence of heaven by looking at the sky. Heaven is what one accepts by faith alone, regardless of external phenomena. Therefore, when Goodman Brown cries, "With Heaven above, and Faith below, I will yet stand firm against the devil!" (10: 82), his resolve has already been undermined by his manifest reliance on appearances. After all, what will he do when he can no longer see heaven? Hawthorne puts him to the test in the very next line by covering the sky with a cloud that will cause him desperation (10: 82).

Finally, Hawthorne subverts Brown's perception by suggesting that it is the product of his own projection. As a number of critics have noted, there is an immediate relationship between Brown's desire to sin and the appearance of his transformed townsmen in the forest: the incipient sinner wants to justify his contemplated indulgence in sin. Indeed, all the characters whom Brown sees in the initial part of his journey, with the exception of the devil, embody powerful restraints which at the outset effectively impede him from the free reign of his desires. Brown admits, for instance, that he could not bear to meet the minister's eye, nor does he wish to break Faith's heart (10: 77-78). As Paul J. Hurley notes, those restraints, "must be destroyed, rationalized away, before total commitment to evil is possible" (413).

Brown's projection of his own evil motives onto others, whom in his naiveté he had always shrouded in purity and revered as models of piety and decorum, effectively serves to annul their imagined reprobation—and thereby to quiet the objections of his own conscience. It is, after all, much easier to sin when one believes that the whole world does it. There is, too, a kind of psychological order to the others' appearance in the forest which evinces Brown's latent mental control. All arrive, for instance, at critical moments when Brown's conscience is in danger of reasserting itself: the appearance of Goody Cloyse saves Brown from a premature bout with his conscience by subtly diverting his attention from Faith—not, of course, without Brown's complicity (10: 78-80); the minister appears only after his name is mentioned as an objection (10: 80-81); and when, in the last ditch, Brown declares, "[W]ith . . . Faith . . . , I will yet stand firm against the devil" (10: 82), the ribbon falls, as if right on cue (10: 83).

Even the devil, as Hurley notes, is a "personal devil" (413), imaginatively domesticated and humanized to appear very much like Brown himself. Whether or not, like David Levin, one reads the devil as an actual being to whom all of the visions or experiences in the forest are attributable, the point is, surely, that, as Michael Colacurcio states, "in Hawthorne's psychological scheme Brown's suspicion and distrust and the devil's wiles are not different" (295). Hawthorne blurs the distinction between self and other in this case by equivocating the origin of the devil's voice: the devil's arguments, he writes, "seemed rather to spring up in the bosom of his auditor, than to be suggested by himself" (10: 80).

Other sensual impressions of Brown's reinforce this pattern of projection. Brown's identification of Martha Carrier is especially significant since it is one of the few cases of positive identification in the story that might presumably give his testimony validity. However, Brown does not see the traces of beauty and the "still majestic . . . figure" (11: 75) that Hawthorne describes in "Main Street," nor does Brown describe her in any individuality of dress or manner. Instead, he declares her a "rampant hag . . . who had received the devil's promise to be queen of hell" (10:86)—inadvertently repeating the exact words that Cotton Mather had used to describe her (qtd. in Burr 144), as if Brown had merely hypostatized Mather's words.

Similarly, the Devil's mass seems a projection of Brown's. The evil hymn Brown hears, which "expressed all that our nature can conceive of sin, and darkly hinted at far more" (10: 85), is a case in point. The observation that a hymn is being sung is not attributable to the narrator, since the narrator simply records Brown's impressions and does not comment explicitly about the reality of events in the forest. Therefore, it must be attributable to Brown, who presumably understands enough of the words to know that the hymn is about sin. Yet, the reader later learns that Brown has understood nothing at all of the hymn, since "unfathomable to mere mortals is the lore of fiends" (10: 85). How, then, does one know that the hymn is about sin? Better yet, how does one know that a hymn is even being sung at all? An alternative explanation offers itself: Brown's imagination is capable of metamorphosing the sound of the wind and endowing it with some infernal significance—it, after all, only "seemed" a hymn (10: 84)— just as his imagination transmutes a rock into an altar or pulpit because of some "rude, natural resemblance" (10: 84), and pine trees, "their tops aflame, their stems untouched" (10: 84), into candles. Hawthorne's choice of pine trees is especially significant since pine needles do not burn with the clear, steady flame of a candle, but rather sputter and smoke greatly, as any woodsman knows. All of these phenomena point to the transformative power of Brown's mind, which Hawthorne suggests exceptionally well in one final display of progressively hyperbolic projections: looking at the contents of a "basin [that] was hollowed, naturally, in the rock," Brown wonders, "Did it contain water, reddened by the lurid light? or was it blood? or, perchance, a liquid flame?" (10: 88).

What Brown perceives in the forest is not surprising in light of his Puritan faith. As an adherent of the Puritan conviction in visible and categorical salvation, Brown is eminently predisposed to view life allegorically, and it is the nature of allegory to turn sensory phenomena into specters and ideal essences. What could be more natural, given Brown's predisposition, than for him to see angels or witches everywhere he looks, or to imagine the unknown (i.e., the dark forest, the Devil's mass) as the antithetical inversion of the everyday reality he knows? Wherever an ideal or spiritual reality takes precedence, every empirical fact will be brought into rigid conformity with it.

However, Brown's interpretive dilemma is also the reader's. Hawthorne's genius in this story is, as we saw earlier, to lure the reader into adopting the same allegorical framework of interpretation as Brown. After all, just as Brown's Calvinist faith presumed empirically to distinguish the elect from the damned, so the reader familiar with allegory expects the Red Cross Knights and Archimagos, and Unas and Duessas, to line up readily in their respective camps in the text. Just as Brown believes that his allegorical interpretation corresponds to and is authorized by God's will (as troubling as that may seem to Brown, given the number of devil-worshippers he discovers), so the reader of "YGB" (at least initially) assumes that an allegorical interpretation corresponds to and is authorized by the narrator's intention (who, for instance, made Faith [the woman] represent faith [the religious belief] by claiming that she was "aptly named"). Both sets of expectations are thwarted, however, by Hawthorne's subtle but progressive subversion of the allegorical framework.

In addition to the ways already discussed, Hawthorne renders the allegorical framework invalid by calling attention to its sheer arbitrariness. For instance, Brown's allegorical readings depend by progressively slenderer threads on the situations which give rise to them until we reach an absurd degree of unrelatedness: a falling "something" in which Brown "beholds"[2] (10: 83) a pink (as if one could distinguish colors in the middle of the night in a dark forest)

---

[2] Hostetler notes "the use of the verb 'beheld' in The Scarlet Letter, in which the narrator specifically argues that the red "A" that Dimmesdale thought he 'beheld' in the sky was primarily a product of his 'guilty imagination'" (228, n12).

ribbon comes for him unequivocally to signify the fall of Faith. As Edwin Honig argues, the crude analogy which "does not lend itself to transformation, negates the allegorical function it was created for" (128).

Hawthorne likewise exploits the tension between the fixed, determinate, essential nature of the allegorical sign and the fluid, ambiguous, evolving nature of experience. In The Scarlet Letter, for instance, Hester ultimately voids her scarlet symbol of its intended ideological value by imbuing it with multiple meanings and continually escaping and transforming the categories in which others attempt to fix her. In the same manner, Brown's identification of his townsmen as witches, or absolute negative values, runs aground over their future conduct and circumstances. For example, Faith's ribbons turn out to be in place back in the town, and she ultimately proves herself to be a good wife to him. Also, the community that he suspected of utter pharisaicalness strangely appears (and since Brown is not the one who sees them, the reader can unquestionably credit the account) in loyal attendance at his funeral. This implies that the others never really come to reject Brown, despite his rejection of them, and that they are capable of a sympathy most unbecoming a community of witches.

Finally, Hawthorne undermines the authority of allegory by dramatizing the way in which the very will to idealization is governed by ulterior motives. As we have seen, desires, both conscious and unconscious, influence Brown's perceptions; the urge to simplify and categorize experience is always attended by what he stands to gain. Brown's desire to sin is especially betrayed by his reaction to the loss of his faith. Although one might expect him to be overcome by the apparent collapse of everything that he has lived by, he takes the occasion instead to celebrate his long-awaited license of indulgence. He laughs "loud and long" (10: 83) and seems to fly off down the trail where Heaven and Faith had detained him scant seconds earlier. Reveling in his newly won freedom, he embarks on a happy orgy of self-gratification whose sexual undertones are unmistakable: "On he flew, among the black pines, brandishing his staff with frenzied gestures . . ."

(10: 84). One can only conclude that he sees and hears what he does because he wants to.

However, Brown's desires are far from innocent. In the context of this story, to see others as witches is hardly attributable to the natural modification of perspective that comes with age, nor is it the inevitable consequence of discovering one's own or others' sin. Motivated, as it is, by the need to discredit others' authority, Brown's perception of them as witches constitutes a covert act of violence, a heinous psychological form of character assassination. Indeed, Brown's reliance on what David Levin was the first to identify as the same type of specter evidence used in the Salem Witch Trials (346-47) is as criminal as the event to which Hawthorne alludes. Elsewhere, such as in "Main Street," Hawthorne denounced similar testimony used to send John and Elizabeth Proctor to the gallows, of whom the narrator recounts the absurd claim that "the laughter of their decayed, cackling voices has been heard at midnight, aloft in the air" (11: 75)—a claim no different in kind than Brown's identification of Faith's voice in a cloud passing overhead. Brown is simply too willing to believe the devil (who is, after all, "the Father of Lies") and too hasty in convincing himself of others' depravity. Like Leonard Doane, Brown's counterpart in "Alice Doane's Appeal" who is deceived by a wizard into misjudging his wife, Brown is guilty of an act that in the latter story Hawthorne clearly finds execrable.

Of course, as readers, we do not share Brown's baser motives. That is, there is nothing tangible that we stand to gain by deeming the other characters to be depraved, except perhaps a perverse pleasure at seeing so many apparently upright and pious saints in secret sin. We generally do, however, share the desire of the understanding for simplification and freedom from doubt. What else could lead one critic to say, "In the absence of any final answer to this problem, I conclude that the witches Goodman Brown saw were genuine?" (Paul W. Miller 260; other critics of a similar persuasion include Harry Levin [27, 54]; Leo B. Levy [381]; and John B. Humma [428], among others). If we, along with

Goodman Brown, continue to read allegorically in a context which no longer supports it—that is, if we mistake the categories of a kind of convenient literary shorthand for the reality itself—is not our judgment in Hawthorne's eyes equally reprehensible? As Sheldon Liebman claims, this story indeed puts us to the test.[3]

Of course, Goodman Brown fails the test. Faith and the rest, naively idealized in one extreme, simply pass to the other extreme in order to account for his newly gained knowledge of sin. The problem is that once he has seen them as witches, he can never return to his more innocent, if more generous, image of them as members of the Elect. He is therefore trapped within the mental image of the world he has created. Faith is the only one for whom he admits a doubt simply because in his eyes she was a prospective, as opposed to a fully communing, witch, and he does not know if she has successfully resisted the devil at his entreaty.

His inability to resolve this doubt lies in the cognitive framework within which he attempts to understand her. There is evidence for supposing her still an angel and a newly converted witch, hence she will never fit either category in a complete and satisfactory manner, and he must spend the rest of his days bouncing her back and forth in unresolved suspicion. "In every case," as Michael Colacurcio argues, "evidence counters evidence—where, Hawthorne implies, only faith can be salutary" (299). Only if Brown could see beyond the narrow conceptual categories of his theology would he realize that she has a bit of both in her, that she contains "contradictions," as Whitman later remarked about himself—that, in fact, humanity is complex and cannot be reduced to a mere essence or idea.

---

[3] While I agree with Liebman that "the tale is directed primarily at the reader, whose task it is to distinguish between appearance and reality by way of determining what happens in the story and why" (157), I disagree that "the reader's attention is drawn to ambiguities which are neither important nor resolvable" (159). It is precisely such "ambiguities" that are the stumbling blocks of the allegorical interpreter.

The reader, too, must deny the either/or allegorical meanings which the story seems to promise at the outset, for they will never satisfactorily fit unless the reader ignores or suppresses vital information. The reader must, too, resist thinking that falling ribbons necessarily mean that one's wife has been unfaithful; in fact, pink ribbons may mean nothing at all, unless there is an allegorical mind nearby that cannot tolerate an empty signifier.[4] Only by leaving the allegorical mind "set" can we understand the story and do justice in our judgments of the other characters.

Brown's lasting, gloomy doubt spells the final failure of allegory as a self-sufficient system of understanding. He cannot apply it practically to his experience without coming up against the problem of contradictory evidence. He cannot apply it, moreover, without significantly—even criminally—transforming the nature of everything around him. And Hawthorne shows here, as elsewhere, that cementing an allegorical idealization onto a human being is fraught with perils. Through a subtle intertextuality of the framework of traditional allegory and the narration of an ironic and skeptical modern consciousness, "YGB" exposes the fatal flaw of the allegorical reader.

---

[4] Leo B. Levy argues that the ribbons are a kind of "fanciful joke" (382) and goes on to list some of the many and varied symbolic meanings which critics have assigned them. However, he himself falls into the trap of interpreting their appearance in the forest as a sign that "Faith has deserted Brown" (387).

Chapter Two

Detection, Imagination, and the Introduction to "The Murders in the Rue Morgue"

The conventional view of what is widely regarded as the first authentic detective story, Poe's "The Murders in the Rue Morgue" (hereafter "MRM"), celebrates the brilliance of Dupin's solution and the apotheosis of his ratiocinative powers. It sees the story's central riddle and game-like economy as paradigmatic of the genre of detective fiction as we know it today. Nevertheless, for many modern critics, the story is flawed: the introduction, especially, seems almost to require an apology. Measured against the strict economy achieved in later classics of the genre, the introduction seems simply unnecessary. The few critics who discuss it at all generally dismiss it as a superfluous retelling of what the story demonstrates so well. Robert A. W. Lowndes's assessment is typical: "Having read it with care, I can assure you that today's reader does not need it at all. There is nothing in it that is not accomplished much better in the course of the story once the story starts" (1). Howard Haycraft similarly dismisses the introduction by contrasting it with the "superior" beginning of "The Purloined Letter" in which there is "no delayed approach to the subject" (20). I believe, though, that the introduction has a much more integral relation to the rest of the story and that it was intended by Poe as a key to the story's interpretation. In its carefully chosen categories and subtle hierarchical oppositions, the introduction asserts a mode of analysis which radically undermines the value of Dupin's solution and challenges the reader to re-evaluate the nature of detection itself.

The introduction attempts no less than an unconventional and sweeping redefinition of analysis. Poe challenges, for instance, the historical assumption that analysis was largely a mathematical process. As Thomas L. Hankins observes in Science and the Enlightenment, "[T]he eighteenth century defined analysis as the method of resolving mathematical problems by reducing them to equations" (20), a sense still pervasive in Poe's day. Poe's introduction can be seen as a polemic intended to dissociate the word from the mathematical lexicon through a carefully elaborated set of opposing terms. Analysis, he argues, although "possibly much invigorated by mathematical study," is nevertheless unjustly applied to mathematics since "to calculate is not in itself to analyze" (4: 146-7). Calculation, or the equivalent of a kind of mathematical reasoning, clearly occupies for Poe a lower rung in the hierarchy of mental powers.

Poe clarifies the distinction between calculation and analysis somewhat problematically by analogy to several games, especially chess and whist. Thus, chess, like math, requires "attention," but not true "acumen"; it is merely "complex," but not "profound" (4: 147). The good chess player may be cunning and calculating, but the analytic whist player goes well "beyond the limits of mere rules" and knows "what to observe" (4: 148). The difference between the two players could be formulated more precisely as the whist player's knowledge (and exploitation) of the psychology of his opponent, as against the chess player's merely logical and mechanistic examination of alternate tactical possibilities.[1] The analyst, for Poe, is the one who "throws himself into the spirit of his opponent"

---

[1] Poe's distinction actually ignores significant psychological factors in chess; masters do in fact study the "style" of their opponents and tend to modify their game accordingly, not to mention the psychological considerations that abound in accepting or refusing a gambit, or offering or taking a poisoned pawn, etc.

and "identifies himself therewith" (4: 147). He knows how to take advantage of all the sources "whence legitimate advantage may be derived," including and especially those which "lie among recesses of thought altogether inaccessible to the ordinary understanding" (4: 148).

Such examples fail, however, to define the real difference between calculation and analysis. For one thing, Poe himself blurs the distinction between the two when he observes that whist, which is the game most "greatly tasking the faculty of analysis," has nonetheless also "long been noted for its influence on what is termed calculating power" (4: 148). However, Poe himself dismisses such games as merely "the most trivial occupations" (4: 146) of the analyst and therefore clearly has more significant examples in mind to define analysis.

It is nevertheless worth noting that even in these examples Poe seeks to minimize the role of logic in analysis. After all, it is not a player's logical ability which enables him to win at cards, for what affords game-winning information, according to Poe, "lies not so much in the validity of the inference as in the quality of the observation" (4: 148). This remark suggests that, for Poe, observation is governed by a different form of understanding than logic, since it precedes that of logical inference altogether. "The necessary knowledge," Poe informs us, "is that of <u>what</u> to observe" (4: 148), but he does not explain how one arrives at such knowledge, which seems to be essentially empathic and irrational. All of these instances serve therefore to privilege a kind of direct intuitive knowledge over the more formally structured and intellectually rigorous ratiocination with which the story is generally associated (e.g., the common practice in collections of Poe's stories of classifying "MRM" as one of the "Tales of Ratiocination").

When Poe describes analysis as a "<u>moral</u> activity" (4: 146; my emphasis), he implies that analysis has more consequential objects than just winning at cards or flaunting one's mental muscles. He invests the act at once with moral consequences and a moral imperative. In the original first paragraph included in the 1841 and 1843 texts, but later dropped from the 1845 edition, Poe had been more explicit about the nature of analysis (perhaps too explicit for the tastes of an author who preferred indirectness over directness). He had stated that analysis "may be described, although not defined, as the capacity for resolving thought into its elements" (4: 289), thereby hinting that the story would be concerned with the study of the human mind. Indeed, Leo Lemay argues that when Poe describes analysis as "that moral activity which <u>disentangles</u>" (4: 146), Poe is referring to the "glorious fascination of psychological investigation" (168), and Lemay's own analysis persuasively demonstrates the story's psychological theme. In the original first paragraph, Poe had indicated, moreover, that the story would self-consciously examine the nature of analysis itself. This theme is still pointed to in what now forms the very first line of the story, in which Poe rather enigmatically observes, "The mental features discoursed of as the analytical are, in themselves, but little susceptible of analysis" (4: 146). What Poe does, in effect, is to begin one mystery by introducing another; that is, he suggests that an even more significant mystery than the one that is apparent at the literal level of the narrative may be the discovery of how we solve mysteries. If the project is admittedly difficult ("little susceptible of analysis"), we should, nevertheless, not be dissuaded from attempting to solve the problem, for, as Poe himself sees fit to quote in the epigram immediately preceding, even seemingly impossible puzzles "are not beyond <u>all</u> conjecture" (4:146). And, as we will see, Poe supplies crucial clues.

The most important clue is the narrator's final distinction between "analysis" and "simple ingenuity," which, he says, is "very strictly analogous" to the difference between the "fancy" and the "imagination" (4: 150). The passage concludes, "[T]he ingenious are always fanciful, and the truly imaginative never otherwise than analytic" (4: 150). Such a pairing is surprising when one recalls how pervasive in the nineteenth century was the assumption of a dichotomy between, on the one hand, scientific thought, with which analysis was associated, and, on the other, artistic thought, which was the realm of the imagination. The word imagination possessed, moreover, a particular romantic denotation which made such an alliance all the more unlikely. Poe wrote several definitions of the difference between "fancy" and "imagination," but perhaps the best formulation is as follows:

> The truth is that the just distinction between the fancy and the imagination (and which is still but a distinction of degree) is involved in the consideration of the mystic. We give this as an idea of our own, altogether. We have no authority for our opinion—but do not the less firmly hold it. The term mystic is here employed in the sense of Augustus William Schlegel, and of most other German critics. It is applied by them to that class of composition in which there lies beneath the transparent upper current of meaning an under or suggestive one. What we vaguely term the moral of any sentiment is its mystic or secondary expression. It has the vast force of an accompaniment in music. This vivifies the air; that spiritualizes the fanciful conception, and lifts it into the ideal. (10: 65)

The critical distinction for Poe, then, is the "mystical," the "suggestive," the "ideal," or the "spiritual" nature of the imagination, as opposed to the merely associative and superficial fancy. Although Poe admits this distinction to be one only of degree, he nevertheless emphasizes that the corresponding difference between ingenuity and analysis is "far greater" than that between "fancy" and "imagination." Poe thereby implies that the ingenious person reads literally and is oblivious to hermeneutic suggestiveness, whereas the true analyst recognizes and articulates figurative levels of meaning. Not surprisingly, Poe's analytical paradigm fits no profession quite so well as that of the creative writer and/or literary critic, the two roles at which he himself most excelled.

When Poe claims that he has "no authority for [his] opinion," he is perhaps masking the debt he owes to a long and profuse tradition of similar distinctions which evolved throughout the eighteenth century and culminated with those of Schelling and Coleridge (see, for example, the detailed list given in James Engell, The Creative Imagination: Enlightenment to Romanticism, 172-

83). Most of the Romantics and a number of their precursors distinguished at least between the lowly, merely mechanical and associative fancy and the higher imagination which through willful control could unify a series of associations into an organic and transcendent whole. Poe was probably familiar with Coleridge's distinction between the fancy which "must receive all its materials ready made from the law of association" and the "secondary imagination" which tries "to idealize and to unify" and "blends, and (as it were) fuses" (202). Indeed, the same process of fusion is discernible in Poe's own description of the catalytic nature of the imagination, for when, according to Poe, the imagination combines "atomic" elements, or "previous combinations" of things, "the admixture of two elements will result in a something that shall have nothing of the quality of one of them— or even nothing of the qualities of either" (16: 156), like a new chemical compound. What is produced is an aesthetic or ethereal quality which he variously labels "beauty," "sublimity," and "harmony," as against the combinations of fancy which may be novel and strike us "as a difficulty happily overcome," but which lack harmony and are "absolutely . . . less beautiful" (12: 39). Imagination thus involves, for Poe, a creative transformation of received materials which finally transcends the sum of its parts, and "even out of deformities it fabricates that Beauty which is at once its sole object and inevitable test" (16: 156).

Of course, for Poe, analysis is not exactly synonymous with the process of artistic fusion or synthesis that he attributed to the creative imagination. Nevertheless, Poe made clear in the original opening paragraph just how closely related the two activities were. He declared, "The processes of invention and creation are strictly akin with the processes of resolution—the former being nearly, if not absolutely, the latter conversed" (4: 289). We should note several things about this statement. First, it defines resolution, or analysis (Poe uses the two terms synonymously here), strictly in terms of an artistic process. Both "invention" and "creation" were favorite bywords of the Romantics, and both refer to imaginative composition, as distinct from the lesser "constructive or combining power" that Poe associated with mere ingenuity. Indeed, Poe approvingly quoted Coleridge's dictum, "The fancy combines, the imagination creates" (10: 61-62), and Floyd Stovall notes that Poe "often used the word 'create' in Coleridge's sense" (161). The terms "invention" and "creation" presuppose a purposeful design or intent and do not refer to spontaneous or accidental combinations or events. Second, the statement describes resolution as almost exactly the converse of the process of imaginative composition. This suggests one of the frequent aims of literary criticism itself, which is to trace a work back to its originating ideas or principles. We must pause to examine this procedure, which is problematic in Poe's thought.

The work of Poe's which best exemplifies his notion of the resolution of a work of art into its constituent elements is the "Philosophy of Composition," in which he sets about in the "interest of an analysis, or reconstruction," to "detail, step by step, the processes by which ["The Raven"] attained its ultimate point of completion" (14: 194-5). The problem with such a mode of analysis, as Poe himself recognized, was that to reduce a work of art to a series of rational steps was invariably to mar its artistic wholeness, or the unity of effect that was attainable only in the reader's total response. In his marginalia, Poe comments precisely on the conflict between these two different modes of knowing:

> To see distinctly the machinery—the wheels and pinions—of any work of Art is, unquestionably, of itself, a pleasure, but one which we are able to enjoy only just in proportion as we do not enjoy the legitimate effect designed by the artist:—and, in fact, it too often happens that to reflect analytically upon Art, is to reflect after the fashion of the mirrors in the temple of Smyrna, which represent the fairest images as deformed. (16: 170)

According to Poe, rational analysis distorts the object of art and precludes true comprehension of the artist's design. Moreover, it can destroy the very beauty of the work, deforming even "the fairest images." Thus, the problem with "The Philosophy of Composition" itself is that it attempts to reduce beauty to "the precision and rigid consequence of a mathematical problem" (14: 195)—or to the very type of mathematical reasoning, or calculation, that is devalued in "The Murders in the Rue Morgue." Although "The Philosophy of Composition" attains in this manner a certain kind of truth, the kind that Poe describes as "the satisfaction of the Reason" (14: 275), it is incapable of arriving at the higher, "loftier," or mystic truth which is revealed only in the total imaginative response of the reader, and which Poe defines, at least with regard to poetry, as "the excitement, or pleasurable elevation, of the soul" (14: 198).

Poe's privileging of holistic imaginative perception is not surprising, given what amounts to his chronic distrust of analytical reason. As David Ketterer notes, Poe saw reason not only as "a barrier to understanding," but also as "an obstacle in the way of ideal perception" (119, 114), a quality which quite obviously placed it in open conflict with the imagination. The introductory part of Eureka, Poe's great and final attempt to vindicate the imagination, takes the form of a full-fledged attack on systematic rational thought. When Poe defines resolution as the converse of imaginative composition, then, he implies a form of understanding that transcends reason and that is capable of an acute perception of the ideal.[2] The process requires an apparently intuitive detection of the author's most profound sense, and it was not supposed to be easy.

Poe did not, after all, like the ideal meaning in literature to be too patent. He deprecated allegory, for instance, on the grounds that it advertised its ideal meaning too obtrusively and appealed at best to the fancy. The ideal meaning in

---

[2] It is interesting to note that, for both Hawthorne and Melville, reason was similarly incapable of apprehending the mystic sign, which communicated itself through a different faculty instead. Upon discovery of the embroidered scarlet letter, for instance, the narrator of "The Custom House" writes, "Certainly, there was some deep meaning in it, most worthy of interpretation, and which, as it were, streamed forth from the mystic symbol, subtly communicating itself to my sensibilities, but evading the analysis of my mind" (1: 31). Likewise, Ishmael, discussing the mystic whiteness of the whale in Moby-Dick, observes, "To analyse it, would seem impossible"; yet, "without imagination no man can follow another into these halls" (192). Indeed, for Melville, the one who most strongly perceives the mystic symbol is the "man of untutored ideality," who is "unread" and "unsophisticated" (192). My thanks to Beverley R. Voloshin for pointing this out.

allegory no doubt seemed too mechanically and arbitrarily managed for Poe's tastes. He preferred instead a subtle suggestiveness in prose, with more of an "intelligible connection" and "effective affinity" between "the real and the unreal" (13: 148). Thus, even Poe could enjoy formal allegory if it were "properly handled, judiciously subdued, seen only as a shadow or by suggestive glimpses, and making its nearest approach to truth in a not obtrusive and therefore not unpleasant appositeness" (13: 149). Curiously, Poe describes the difference between allegory and what we might label "judicious suggestiveness" as, at least in part, the degree to which the reader's participation is required in perceiving the ideal meaning, as opposed to the reader's being, as it were, bashed over the head with it. Poe states, "Where the suggested meaning runs through the obvious one in a very profound undercurrent so as never to interfere with the upper one without our own volition, so as never to show itself unless called to the surface, there only, for the proper uses of fictitious narrative, is it available at all" (13: 148). This statement reveals Poe's awareness of the need for the ideal meaning actively to be called up or evoked by the reader—a meaning which would otherwise remain hidden beneath the literal sense.

Similarly, Poe suggests elsewhere that the full effect of a piece of fiction ultimately depends on the reader's reciprocal effort in producing it. In a discussion of the principal of unity of effect, Poe states, "[B]y such means, with such care and skill, a picture is at length painted which leaves in the mind of him who contemplates it with a kindred art, a sense of the fullest satisfaction" (11: 108; my emphasis). It is significant that Poe should employ the term art as a description of reading, for it denotes both an active engagement and consummatable proficiency. It is, moreover, a "kindred" art—that is, one which matches the artist's own esoteric art—and clearly, an inordinate effort would be necessary to fathom the artistic design of a brilliant creative imagination such as Poe's. The reader who would reveal the "analytical promptings of that poetic genius which, in its supreme development, embodies all orders of intellectual capacity" (16: 129), must be capable of the same sophisticated degree of analysis himself. Perhaps that is why Poe once commented that the reader who truly appreciates the author's intended effect fancies that he or she and the author "have, together, created this thing" (13: 146). We may also note that the "fullest satisfaction" which Poe describes as attending a successful reading is very much like the "liveliest enjoyment" that the analyst is supposed to derive from analysis in "MRM."

Poe's redefinition of analysis as an act of imagination marks the story's thematic concern with the categories of thought and of epistemology. It indicates, too, how we are to read the main body of the narrative. Poe emphasizes the thematic continuity between the introduction and the narrative proper by declaring that the latter will be somewhat like "a commentary upon the propositions just advanced" (4: 150). This I take to mean that the narrative should be read as an illustration and explication of Poe's introductory antithesis between true analysis (imagination) and the various lower forms of rational understanding (calculation, ingenuity, etc.) that constrict themselves to purely literal, superficial, or factual meaning. In this manner, Poe polemically affirms the power of the imagination not only against mathematical reasoning, but against the other aspects of Enlightenment thought that the Romantics wished to repudiate, which, according to Engell, included "materialistic theories of mind and body, and atomistic philosophy" (5). Poe rejected such doctrines because they granted ultimate authority to facts alone and thus denied the reality of an ideal, mystic, or transcendent truth available only to the imagination. However, in exclusively championing the imagination, Poe was simultaneously condemning Dupin, the arch-positivist in whom the worst excesses of rationalism are united.

Let me parenthetically state that my claim is limited only to Dupin's treatment in "MRM," in which, as I intend to show, Dupin embodies positivistic and rational, hence, unimaginative thought. This is notably not true of "The Purloined Letter," in which Dupin is actually portrayed for the first time as a poet and thus, in a curious reversal, as the spokesman for the imagination. Although readers tend to think of Dupin as a consistent character throughout the three stories in which he appears, Dupin's role actually varies significantly, much like that of Gulliver in Gulliver's Travels. For instance, in "MRM," Dupin is the paragon of rational method, and he criticizes the Parisian police for having "no method in their proceedings, beyond the method of the moment" (4: 165). In "The Purloined Letter," the situations are exactly reversed: it is the police who are dogmatically methodical and who "have no variation of principle in their investigations" (6: 42) while Dupin adapts his method to the contingencies of the moment. Moreover, in "MRM," Dupin's analysis is eminently spatial and quantitative: not only does he determine the mode of ingress and egress of the murderer and infer the kind of creature in part from the kind of acrobatic agility it would need to enter the room, but he also typically solves problems by breaking them down into smaller parts and studying individual details such as the nail, the sailor's ribbon, and the patch of orangutan hair in order to reconstruct the whole. Yet, this same principle of spatial and quantitative analysis is precisely what is parodied in "The Purloined Letter," in which the Prefect becomes ridiculous with his superfluous array of microscopes and long probing needles, as well as his futile division of space into "the fiftieth part of a line" (6: 34). The differences in Poe's depiction of Dupin from one story to the next evince Poe's changing rhetorical designs.

Poe suggests (and one should remember how important suggestion is in a tale that defines imagination as the perception of a suggestive undercurrent of meaning) Dupin's positivism in a number of ways. Dupin is portrayed, for instance, as having a scientific mind. He is well versed in "nebular cosmogony" (4: 155), and he practices the classical scientific method of analysis; that is, he formulates hypotheses and then tests them empirically by predicting and verifying each of the narrator's reactions in turn. There is, too, a notable element of what Poe disparagingly calls calculation, or mathematical reasoning, in Dupin's thought. For instance, Dupin enthusiastically endorses the "theory of probabilities—that theory to which the most glorious objects of human research are indebted for the most glorious of illustration" (4: 179), and he employs calculation in the process of identifying the murderer, such as in his determination of the unlikelihood of finding Asiatics or Africans in Paris (4: 171).

Dupin's approving reference to Epicurus as "that noble Greek" (4: 155) suggests, moreover, the affinity of Dupin's thought to both empiricism and atomism. Epicurus, who was perhaps the first declared empiricist, founded his philosophical system on the infallibility of sense experience. He rejected all transcendent truth claims and sought to refute idealism by basing all knowledge solely on hard facts. He was also particularly harsh on the language of poetry and myth which he felt only obscured meaning and confused thought (P. H. De Lacy 3). Therefore, to the extent that Dupin endorses Epicurus's views, he necessarily demonstrates his own ironic distance from Poe's. Furthermore, Epicurus's atomism was based on a mechanistic conception of causality: he believed that atoms falling through space would eventually coalesce and form not only the natural configurations of this world but also the gods themselves, who were not the source, but only the products of creation. Even the human soul was supposed to be composed of atoms. Atomic theory was thus a set of purely physical laws, and it described a universe whose principle of order lay solely in the sequence of changes in the combinations of its atoms. A similar mechanistic bias is observable in Dupin's reading of the narrator's thoughts. He is interested in them, after all, only as a causal chain of individual facts, much as one would enjoy predicting the order of a series of falling dominos. In effect, Dupin's analysis reduces the narrator to a curious machine whose inner workings are to be charted solely for the scientific interest of the activity. Dupin's interest in the two murders is likewise limited solely to material concerns, such as the identity of the criminal and the mode of ingress and egress from the room.

Poe indicates further shortcomings in Dupin when the latter mentions "stereotomy" and "atomies" (4: 155), two terms which resonate far more deeply with respect to Dupin's way of thinking than that of the narrator's, to whom Dupin attributes them. Stereotomy, which is the science or art of cutting or making sections of solids, reduces things to fragments and particles, or "atomies." As an analytical science it is, like atomism and positivism, founded on the assumption that the nature of the whole can be discovered by dividing it into its component parts and studying each part by itself. This is, of course, precisely Dupin's procedure, who in "MRM" breaks problems down into a series of logical steps and examines each piece of evidence closely. Although Dupin criticizes Vidocq for "impair[ing] his vision by holding the object too close" (4: 166), it is ironically Dupin himself who examines with a "minuteness of attention" (4: 167), who "scrutinize[s] everything" (4: 168), and who labors over "atomies," or small details, such as the broken nail, the lack of syllabification in the shrill voice, and the sailor's ribbon.[3] Similarly, Dupin impeaches himself when he observes that Vidocq "might see, perhaps, one or two points with unusual clearness, but in so doing he, necessarily, lost sight of the matter as a whole" (4: 166), for it is Dupin who loses sight of the matter as a whole—as an imaginative, holistic whole, that is.

Dupin fails to perceive the ideal precisely because he is obsessed by the material fact, the particular detail. When Dupin claims, for instance, that "in investigations such as we are now pursuing, it should not be so much asked 'what has occurred,' as 'what has occurred that has never occurred before'" (4: 169), he is arguing against an ideal understanding, or what we might call the timeless truths of the human heart—for murder is as old as the human race. His statement

---

[3] When, in a letter to Poe, Philip Cooke criticized Dupin as being "too minute & hair-splitting" (17: 263), Poe responded with a strangely enthusiastic endorsement of his friend's comment; he wrote, "Were I in a serious humor just now, I would tell you frankly how your words of appreciation make my nerves thrill—not because you praise me (for others have praised me more lavishly) but because I feel that you comprehend and discriminate. You are right about the hair-splitting of my French friend:—that is all done for effect" (17: 265). It is too bad that Poe was not more explicit about the nature of the effect that he intended, but he seems very happy that someone had finally seen through Dupin, for it is his friend's critical remarks that Poe commends.

emphasizes instead the importance of the local contours or configurations of such an event, the specific material accidents of time and place. He affirms, in other words, the importance of detail.

Yet, Poe distrusted detail as a path toward truth. He believed that what was distinct was usually deceptive (Ketterer 30) and that details only served to distort the understanding. Notice, for instance, his condemnatory remarks in Eureka: "The error of our progenitors was quite analogous with that of the wiseacre who fancies he must necessarily see an object the more distinctly, the more closely he holds it to his eyes. They blinded themselves, too, with the impalpable, titillating Scotch snuff of detail" (16: 190). Poe advocated seeking truth not with microscopic precision, but with macrocosmic imprecision. He called for "a mental gyration on the heel" atop Mount Etna in order to bring about "so rapid a revolution of all things about a central point of sight that, while the minutiae vanish altogether, even the more conspicuous objects become blended into one" (16: 187). Only by means of such a distant and kaleidoscopic perception—a metaphor for the imagination—could humanity transcend detail and arrive at an apprehension of unity, or of the ideal.

Strangely enough, the narrator, who "cannot possibly understand the particulars of this frightful mystery" (4: 182), is by that very reason the one closest to feeling Poe's notion of ideal effect. The narrator's response is direct and intuitive and not led astray by logical vivisection. It is characterized, too, by its emotional intensity, another important component for Poe in the perception of the ideal. As Lemay notes, Poe had a "fundamental ontological belief that emotions guided the reason—and even that emotions were truer than reason" (175). Poe expresses such a preference by dedicating Eureka "to those who feel rather than to those who think" (16: 183). The narrator is thus able to perceive things to which Dupin is blinded by the exclusively intellectual nature of his understanding.

The narrator is, for instance, able to sense a vague aura of horror in the details of the crime. Despite Dupin's carefully orchestrated attempt to impress the narrator with his tour de force of logical reasoning, it is, ironically, the unintentionally suggestive portions of Dupin's narrative to which the latter most responds. He experiences a "shudder" (4: 168) and a "creeping of the flesh" (4: 181) as Dupin reviews the peculiar aspects of the evidence. Such a response is significant, since, in accord with Poe's theory of unity of effect, it serves to bring the reader either consciously or unconsciously into tune with the mystic or metaphorical sense of Dupin's words. As Lemay states, "[T]he thoughts of the reader are precisely guided and verbalized by the narrator, who functions as the reader/audience within the story" (176). And what the narrator ultimately awakens us to, according to Lemay, is the perverse sexual nature of the crime (176-79).

Dupin fails to perceive this deeper significance because, like the supposedly dispassionate scientist, he relies solely on his rational intellect to guide him. Poe suggests, however, that there is something unbalanced in Dupin's extreme emotional detachment: "His manner at these moments was frigid and abstract; his eyes were vacant in expression" (4: 152). How odd that just when Dupin's object is to read men through the "windows in their bosoms" (4:152), he should be so remote from his own heart! The words, "frigid," "abstract," and "vacant," suggest an utter absence of feeling and a completely schizophrenic dissociation from the unconscious, irrational, and latently hysterical part of himself. This split is further evinced by Dupin's two voices, which are shown to be aspects of his mental processes. It is, for instance, only during the exercise of his "peculiar analytic ability" that "his voice, usually a rich tenor, rose into a treble which would have sounded petulantly but for the deliberateness and entire distinctness of the enunciation" (4: 152). Although Dupin succeeds in "The Purloined Letter" by virtue of an "identification of [his] intellect with that of his opponent" (6: 41), we cannot imagine him making the same identification with the brute frenzy of the orangutan in "MRM" or, as the schoolboy suggests, fashioning the expression of his face in accordance with the ape's and waiting to see "what thoughts or sentiments arise" (6: 41).

The orangutan represents, in fact, precisely what Dupin represses in his thinking—and what is shown to gain in explosive potential in direct proportion to the degree of its repression: it is, in Lemay's words, "the reality and power of libidinous drives" (179). That this orangutan is meant to perform a metaphorical rather than verisimilar function is shown by the very implausibility of its behavior. In fact, this is no ordinary or natural orangutan, and Poe's narrator only misleads the reader when he declares that "the wild ferocity . . . of these mammalia are sufficiently well known to all" (4: 182). In reality, Poe's source, Cuvier, described the orangutan in exactly the opposite manner as "gentle and easily domesticated" (43), in light of which its brutal and ferocious behavior in this tale is virtually unthinkable.

Such behavior would not, however, be unthinkable in its more civilized counterpart. In fact, Poe slyly points to the orangutan's metaphorical function by mentioning its "imitative propensities" (4: 182). According to Lemay, the orangutan not only imitates, but is actually a double for, its French master, the proverbial sailor in port associated with unrestrained sexuality and animality (182). In this manner, Poe suggests that the mangling and decapitation of the two female bodies in the story is actually prompted by an all too human motive. It is the ability to conceive of—and even, imaginatively, to share—this motive, that makes the narrator's skin creep as he listens to Dupin recount the details.

This vague, suggestive sense of horror is, however, precisely what Dupin's solution eliminates. Surely, Poe throws us off the scent when the narrator, upon discovering the killer to be an orangutan, declares, "I understood the full horrors of the murder at once" (4: 182). Given the mutilated state of the bodies and the awful agony that the narrator already knows the L'Espanayes to have undergone, what added horror could there be in discovering that the perpetrator was an orangutan acting blindly and by instinct? The real horror is to imagine—as the narrator does when he guesses that a maniac had done the deed—that there was some perverse but recognizably human pleasure in the act. Such a pleasure is more than amply hinted at by the numerous sexual innuendoes in the tale, but it is especially revealed by the guilt that it immediately gives rise to in the orangutan—a guilt that is also remarkably human: "Conscious of having deserved punishment, it seemed desirous of concealing its bloody deeds, and skipped about the chamber in an agony of nervous agitation; throwing down and breaking the furniture as it moved, and dragging the bed from the bedstead" (4: 190-91). Just how aware the orangutan is of having willfully done wrong is hinted at by the scope of its subsequent fear of retribution. In its attempt to hide the evidence of its recent carnage, the orangutan hurls one of the bodies through the window and thrusts the other up the chimney "so forcibly that the united vigor of several persons was found barely sufficient to bring it down" (4: 179-80). Under the circumstances, what greater confession of wrongdoing could it make?

However, the ultra-rational Dupin goes so far as to deny the idea of a motive altogether. Like Epicurus, who posited a natural swerve in the atoms that was blind, spontaneous, and not subject to necessity, Dupin, in a way, merely sees the orangutan as a chance-like element that suddenly and spontaneously irrupts into the L'Espanayes' apartment and dismembers them. The overall effect of his analysis is implicitly to negate all moral responsibility for the murders and utterly to diminish their significance. In fact, Dupin treats the enigma of the murders as he would a riddle or any trivial exercise; he remarks that an inquiry into the murders "will afford [him and the narrator] amusement" (4: 167; my emphasis)—a term which even the narrator has the delicacy to recognize is odd in such a context.

Dupin seems, indeed, incapable of identifying with the L'Espanayes' suffering, but then sympathy, or what we might today term "empathy," was widely regarded as a power of the imagination (see especially Engell 143-60).

Even Dupin's notion of tragedy is intellectual and dispassionate. For instance, he agrees with the narrator in the introduction that Chantilly's diminutive figure "unfitted him for tragedy" (4: 153), as if physical stature itself determined tragic sentiment. He reduces tragedy to a mere form by his inability to feel anything at all for the shocking and catastrophic end of the L'Espanayes, an event which even the newspaper, criticized elsewhere by Dupin, has the sense—or rather the feeling—to refer to as the "tragedy in the Rue Morgue" (4: 158).

Dupin's purely intellectual treatment of the murders is symptomatic of a profound psychological imbalance. He is, indeed, first described as a man who has retreated away from the world and into himself, after having been "reduced to such poverty that the energy of his character succumbed beneath it" (4: 150). Dupin lives a life of the mind, indulging himself only in the luxury of books. He is associated with decay, impotence, and death by inhabiting a "time-eaten and grotesque mansion . . . tottering to its fall in a retired and desolate portion of the Faubourg St. Germain" (4: 151). Further, the narrator's admission, "We existed within ourselves alone" (4: 151), denotes an unnatural severance not only from the life of the community, but from the life of the body as well. Dupin has even altered the natural cycles of sleep and waking, substituting a couple of tapers, "which threw out the ghastliest and feeblest of rays" (4: 151) for the life-supporting energies of the sun, and transforming his daytime hours into "dreams" (4: 151).

The narrator hints at the truth in the introduction when he writes, "Had the routine of our life at this place been known to the world, we should have been regarded as madmen" (4: 151). Likewise, he later speculates that Dupin's peculiar analytic ability was perhaps the result of a "diseased intelligence" (4: 152). In fact, judging by Poe's own definition, Dupin exhibits the single definitive trait that not only precludes him from being considered a true genius, but which also eminently qualifies him in Poe's eyes as a victim of madness:

[A]nalysis of mental power . . . [teaches] that <u>highest</u> genius . . . is but the result of generally large mental power existing in a state of <u>absolute proportion</u>—so that no one faculty has undue prominence. <u>That</u> factitious 'genius'—that 'genius' in the popular sense—which is but the manifestation of the abnormal predominance of some one faculty over all the others—and, of course, at the expense and to the detriment, of all the others—is a result of mental disease or rather, of organic malformation of mind. . . . [S]uch genius . . . will give unmistakeable [sic] indications of <u>unsoundness</u>. (14: 176-7)

As we have seen, Dupin displays just such a marked lack of mental proportion, and his denial of the body and of the emotions provides "unmistakeable indications of unsoundness." He is thus suggestively implicated in the murders by the narrator's suggestion that it was a madman who had committed the crime.

Lemay demonstrates that Dupin is incriminated in the murders by means of his symbolic relation to the other characters. According to Lemay, the characters form three sets of doubles, of which "Dupin and the narrator represent the analyzing and creative intelligence—aspects of reason; the L'Espanayes represent the suppression of the emotions—another aspect of the head's supremacy; and the orangutan and the sailor represent animality and sexuality—the body alone" (188). (Although Lemay is essentially right about the characters' symbolic relations, I would nevertheless modify his use of terminology, since I believe the terms "analyzing and creative intelligence" that he attributes to Dupin and the narrator are reserved by Poe to designate true imagination.) Thus, it is symbolically significant that Madam L'Espanaye's head is severed from her body, for, as Dupin's double, she vividly portrays his failure to integrate thought and feeling. Moreover, Lemay shows that it is the repressive nature of Dupin's intellect which is itself ultimately responsible for the crime. In the symbolic logic of the tale, the fury of the orangutan's passion is equaled only by the degree of the emotional repression which gives rise to it, like a match placed within the accumulated fumes of a gas oven. And if Dupin's intellect is what symbolically causes the murders, it is also the very thing that blinds him to his implication in them.

Poe underscores Dupin's failure to understand the real nature of the murders by means of a series of accusations that Dupin makes against the Prefect in the story's conclusion. Although intending to criticize the Prefect's analytical faults, Dupin ironically reveals his own instead. He has, for instance, shown himself to be merely "cunning" and not "profound," since "cunning," in Poe's usage belongs to ingenuity, and profundity to the imagination. In fact, Dupin specifically argues against profundity—and, hence, against the imagination— when he claims, "Truth is not always in a well. In fact, as regards the more important knowledge, I do believe that she is invariably superficial" (4: 166). It is, moreover, his own wisdom which lacks "stamen," or a sexual dimension, just as it is his he himself who "is all head and no body" (4: 192). His final comment that the Prefect has a way "de nier ce qui est, et d'explique ce qui n'est pas" (4: 192; or "of denying what is, and of explaining what is not") is especially ironic since the Prefect has neither denied nor explained anything in the course of the tale! It is rather Dupin himself who denies what is and explains what is not. For example, Dupin characteristically proclaims at one point that "Madame and Mademoiselle L'Espanaye were not destroyed by spirits" (4: 172), although clearly in a metaphorical sense they were—and it is with those other senses that Poe's true analyst is interested.

In the strict terms of the introduction, then, Dupin does not prove himself capable of true analysis, but only of "simple ingenuity." That is, he identifies a material ape, but fails entirely to apprehend its mystical significance. Poe also plays with a less common, now obsolete meaning of ingenuity as "ingenuousness" or "innocence" (supported by a second but similar sense of the word "simple" in the same phrase)—Dupin, the innocent, cannot imagine that the motive for the crime could have been sexual in nature.

The reader must also guard against displaying ingenuity and against being "simple."[4] In other words, the reader must guard against the innocence or artlessness of reading for literal truth and of taking appearances at face value. The reader must not be duped by August Dupin[g], Poe's most convincing hoax. The introduction is, in fact, an implicit challenge to the reader to prove him- or herself capable of analysis, that is, to be skeptical of superficial truths and alive to the metaphorical potential of language. And in its implicit hierarchy of readers and revelation of the proper modus operandi, Poe's introductory analysis turns out to be an analogue for literary detection itself.

---

[4] Poe complained in a letter to Philip Cooke that "the reader is made to confound the ingenuity of the suppositious Dupin with that of the writer of the story" (17: 112). It is significant that he singles out "MRM" to criticize in the same letter, for Poe clearly identified with Dupin much more in "The Mystery of Marie Roget," in which he later included a footnote proudly taking credit for having solved the real-life case.

Chapter Three

"Benito Cereno" and the American Confidence Man

Perhaps Melville's chief problem as an artist, especially after the publication of Mardi, was the vast and mounting gulf between what he wanted to write and what his readers wanted to read. Melville's exotic romances sold well, but whenever he moved experimentally into allegory or metaphysical speculation, such as in Mardi and Moby-Dick, the sales dropped, and he was driven back to what he came to regard as his literary hack work.[1] Melville memorably expressed this conflict in a famous letter to Hawthorne written on 1 June 1851:

> Dollars damn me; and the malicious Devil is forever grinning in upon me, holding the door ajar. . . . What I feel most moved to write, that is banned,—it will not pay. Yet, altogether, write the other way I cannot. So the product is a final hash, and all my books are botches. (Correspondence, 191)

---

[1] All of Melville's early novels that had a preponderance of exotic adventure and a minimum of both philosophy and allegory enjoyed successful sales. For example, in two years Typee went into three editions and sold over 5,000 copies (Howard 128), and the first edition of Omoo (over 3,000 copies) sold out in a week. After the unsuccessfully experimental Mardi, which took seven years to sell 3,000 copies (Charvat 49), Melville returned to his more popular, formulaic work in Redburn and White-Jacket, each of which had a brisk sales of more than 4,000 copies in a matter of months (Howard 151, 153). The sales of his greatest work, Moby Dick, were, in comparison, meager: 2,500 copies in five years and only 500 more during the next fifteen years (Charvat 41).

Like so many other artists, Melville sought to sell books and to preserve his artistic integrity.

The problem was exacerbated by what Melville came to see as unwillingness in his compatriots to face the dark truth about themselves and about life, and he increasingly railed against the constrictions of popular taste and morality, as he does in "Hawthorne and His Mosses":

> [I]n this world of lies, Truth is forced to fly like a scared white doe in the woodlands; and only by cunning glimpses will she reveal herself, as in Shakespeare and other masters of the great Art of Telling the Truth—even though it be covertly, and by snatches. (Piazza, 244)

In the same vein, he had written to Hawthorne:

> Truth is the silliest thing under the sun. Try to get a living by the Truth—and go to the Soup Societies. Heavens! Let any clergyman try to preach the Truth from its very stronghold, the pulpit, and they would ride him out of his church on his own pulpit banister. (Correspondence, 191)

When Melville finally sought to express his frustration openly in Pierre, the work in which he indulged in his most unrestrained outbursts against both readers and critics alike, the attempt almost sealed his fate as a popular writer. Pierre was a dismal financial failure; it took 35 years to sell 1800 copies (Charvat 51). The experience only served to heighten the crisis for Melville.

Melville found one solution to this dilemma in the work of Hawthorne, whom he had praised in 1850 in "Hawthorne and His Mosses" for the latter's ability to "hoodwink" (Piazza, 250) the world. Melville observed that Hawthorne was able to weave the dark truth into his work in such a way that not every reader would discern it, "for it is, mostly, insinuated to those who may best understand it, and account for it; it is not obtruded upon every one alike" (Piazza, 245). With obvious interest for his own evolving modus operandi, Melville noted, "[I]t is certain, that some of them [Hawthorne's tales] are directly calculated to deceive— egregiously deceive, the superficial skimmer of pages" (Piazza, 251).

Hawthorne's singular ability to write serious fiction and still sell books seemed to hold out the promise of similar success to Melville. Although Melville himself wrote for "the eagle-eyed reader" (Piazza, 251), the ideal of readerly perspicuity and sympathy that seemed for him at times to find its physical embodiment in Hawthorne[2], he nevertheless knew that he had to appeal to the far more numerous—and financially sustaining—superficial skimmers of pages.

Although Melville became increasingly deceptive in his novels, he had his greatest success with this rhetorical strategy in the shorter magazine pieces of the 1850s—in which, as William Charvat notes, Melville indeed "did some of the darkest and bitterest writing of his life" (55). In one of those pieces, "Benito Cereno" (hereafter "BC"), which to my mind is the pre-eminent masterpiece of The Piazza Tales, Melville succeeds so well in deceiving his readers that the novella has been widely misunderstood only until recently. Actually, the novella is as scathingly critical of Americans and of American values as anything Melville wrote; what is different about it is that the dark truth "is not obtruded upon everyone alike" for it is designed innocuously to appeal to the very group of readers that it effectively condemns. Although much has been written on "BC," no one has yet examined the novella from this point of view. I believe not only that "BC" constitutes the finest example of Melville's deceptive rhetorical strategy in action, but that it also provides the best evidence of his intentions in this regard, which can be more readily ascertained by examining the specific alterations he made to his source, Amasa Delano's Narrative of Voyages. In this chapter, I will analyze Melville's rhetoric strategy by examining how he first develops and then covertly undermines sympathy for Captain Delano.

---

[2] Witness, for instance, the intoxicating effect even of Hawthorne's guarded praise of Moby Dick on Melville, who replied, "A sense of unspeakable security is in me this moment, on account of your having understood the book" (Correspondence, 212).

Melville's revision of his source reveals a consistent design to render Delano as apparently innocent, benign, and reassuringly rooted in middle-class American values as possible, even as Melville subtly but inexorably incriminates him in evil. Melville employs a wide variety of techniques in order to do so. First among these is the care he takes in establishing Delano's sincerity. In dialogues and interior monologues, Delano, the "honest seaman" (86), never consciously lies to anyone, nor does he display any obvious discrepancy between the way he thinks and acts. Indeed, if Delano frankly answers even Cereno's pointedly suspicious questions about his ship's arms and the whereabouts of his men (65-66), how much less likely does it seem that he would ever lie to the reader! Unlike the historical Amasa Delano, who by his own account was actively contending against a possible mutiny and showed far more understanding of human duplicity (see especially Delano 320-21), Melville's Delano is described both as a man of "singular guilelessness" (67) and "a man of such native simplicity as to be incapable of satire or irony" (63). His sheer ingenuousness seems especially calculated to disarm the reader's suspicion.

No doubt Delano's temperament is designed to make readers well disposed toward him as well. In emphasizing Delano's good will and amiability, for instance, Melville adds to his source such adjectives as "blithe" (71), "genial" (84), "pleasant" (71), and "benign" (84). In fact, Melville's Delano exhibits an almost paternal benevolence toward his subordinates, preferring to think of them as a "comfortable family of a crew" (54) rather than merely as bonded labor. Quick to forgive others, he is also quick to chide himself when he thinks he has been in the wrong. He displays an especially winning way of making fun of himself, calling himself "sappy Amasa" (86) and lecturing himself like a child for having entertained unkind suspicions about Cereno: "Fie, fie, Jack of the Beach! you are a child indeed; a child of the second childhood, old boy; you are beginning to dote and drule, I'm afraid. . . . What a donkey I was" (77). It is hard not to like such good-natured self-deprecation.

In addition, Melville's Delano is highly sentimental. He responds with immediate pleasure to the sight of a negress kissing her baby (73), as well as to "the beauty of that relationship [between Cereno and Babo] which could present such a spectacle of fidelity on the one hand and confidence on the other" (57). Delano thus articulates and embodies the values of Melville's Victorian reading public. What matter if in both cases he is duped? (After all, the reader learns later that "the negresses . . . were knowing to the revolt" [112], and since the mother picks up the baby and smothers it in maternal transports only after she sees Delano looking at her, the sequence suggests that her act is not spontaneous but rather cynically calculated to place him off his guard.) Sentimentality can be a powerful and disarming literary tool, as Dickens dramatically showed, and Melville employs it to cloak many a sin, even Delano's implicit approval of slavery.

Melville increases sympathy for Delano by casting him as the apparent advocate of responsible authority. Delano is thus endowed with a love of "good order" (52). He extols "the quiet orderliness" of his ship (54) and decries the disorder and noisy confusion that "repeatedly challenged his eye" (54) on the San Dominick. Delano also seems a committed advocate of justice, for he is quick to denounce two prominent breaches of discipline involving a white boy who is wounded in the head by a knife (59) and a white sailor who is dashed to the deck by two blacks whom he had accidentally incommoded (70). In addition, Delano doles out the food to whites and blacks alike with "republican impartiality" (80) and later saves a number of blacks from the vengeance of certain Spanish sailors (114). Delano seems, indeed, a paragon of justice and humanitarianism.

Melville's Delano also appeals (at least superficially) to the nationalism of American readers. Clearly, American readers identify more with Delano precisely because he is American—because, that is, he represents the known and familiar in a milieu in which the reader, as much as Delano, is at sea. But Melville heightens this identification by kindling a consummate suspicion of everyone foreign, whom he portrays as potentially sinister and threatening. Indeed, Melville brilliantly manipulates the reader's point of view in such scenes as Delano gingerly ascending the ladder between the two rows of ominous-looking hatchet-polishers—is it only Delano who experiences the "apprehensive twitch in the calves of his legs" (59)? Likewise, when Delano "with clenched jaw and hand" and burgeoning fears for his life rushes out of the cabin "from darkness to light," what reader is not relieved to see him finally "unharmed in the light?" (96). This strong visceral identification with Delano is enhanced by his portrayal as the (seemingly) innocent victim of some dark foreign conspiracy.

Other images, too, equate treachery or duplicity with what is foreign and unknown. The sun, for instance, is compared at the outset to a "Lima intriguante's one sinister eye peering across the Plaza from the Indian loop-hole of her dusk saya-y-manta" (47), and Delano recalls accounts of the treacherous practices of Malay pirates, who lure sailors "by the spectacle of thinly manned or vacant decks, beneath which prowled a hundred spears with yellow arms ready to upthrust them through the mats" (68). Likewise, references to Spaniards, as well as to Catholicism, often promote distrust.[3] Delano's first view of the San Dominick reveals, for example, "a ship-load of monks," in which "were what really seemed, in the hazy distance, throngs of dark cowls; while, fitfully revealed through the open port-holes, other dark moving figures were dimly descried, as of Black Friars pacing the cloisters" (48). The repetition of "dark" and emphasis on

---

[3] Melville no doubt was playing to the strongly anti-Catholic element of his contemporary northern reading public by means of a series of slurs against Catholicism, which was at once the national religion of Spain and the ideology that officially justified Spain's colonization of the new world. Given the extent of anti-Catholic sentiment evinced by the electoral success of the Know-Nothing party in the elections of 1854 and 1855, Delano's liberal Protestantism was bound to seem more familiar and acceptable to most readers.

the limitation of sight ("hazy," "fitfully revealed," "dimly") are suggestive of something secret and hidden, even ominous. Later, Delano more bluntly reflects that "as a nation . . . these Spaniards are all an odd set; the very word Spaniard has a curious, conspirator, Guy-Fawkish twang to it" (79). Such descriptions both encourage xenophobia and strengthen the reader's identification with Delano.

As the representative of American culture, Melville's Delano likewise gains by juxtaposition with Hispanic culture, which is systematically denigrated. Cereno, is consistently referred to, for example, as "the Spaniard" (51-55, 57-61, 63-65, 67-70, and passim) as if his own weakness and temperamental defects were metonymically representative of those of his entire race: thus, he is described as "dreary, spiritless" (51), "distempered" (52), "deject[ed]" (52), "sour and gloomy" (53), "disdain[ful]" (53), "splenetic" (53), "proud" (53), "moody" (53), "apathetic" (53), "vindictive" (63), and "morbidly sensitive" (63). He is compared not only to Charles V of Spain but also to a "hypochondriac abbot" with an "unstrung" and "absent or moody mind" (52). Allan Moore Emery has shown that in the mid-1850s such traits were indeed popularly associated with the Spanish, whom the American press stereotypically portrayed as "weak," "despotic," and "disorderly," in contrast to American "energy," "libertarianism," and "efficiency" (50).[4] That Delano exemplifies the latter qualities is shown by, among other things, his impeccable work ethic. He doubtless keeps a trim and tidy ship, for the first thing he notices on approaching the <u>San Dominick</u> is the "slovenly neglect" (48) that pervades it. His coolly critical eye fastens on the fact that "[t]he spars, ropes, and great part of the bulwarks, looked woolly, from long unacquaintance with the scraper, tar, and the brush" (48), and he continually

---

[4] Melville was no doubt playing to the strongly anti-Catholic element of his contemporary northern reading public by means of a series of slurs against Catholicism, which was at once the national religion of Spain and the ideology that had officially justified Spain's colonization of the new world. Given the extent of anti-Catholic sentiment evinced by the electoral success of the Know-Nothing Party in the elections of 1854 and 1855, Delano's liberal Protestantism was bound to seem more familiar and acceptable to most readers.

registers the sad state of deterioration into which the <u>San Dominick</u> has fallen. Moreover, Delano is an energetic commander who will not tolerate idleness. He proudly recounts having once kept a crew thrumming mats for three days during a life-threatening gale (59-60). Delano is also made to seem superior by contrast to the blacks in the novella, who alternately appear, on the one hand, docile, "cheerful" (83), and "stupid" (75)—the common stereotype of the mid-nineteenth century—and, on the other, "ferocious [and] piratical" (99).[5] Such foils serve to enhance the reader's confidence in Delano, the embodiment of Yankee values.

Finally, Melville's Delano displays generosity in his judgment of others. He seems virtually unwilling to think badly about anyone, even in the ugliest and most suspicious circumstances, unless he is absolutely warranted in doing so. Indeed, he will doubt his own perception sooner than conclude something unflattering about someone else, for he believes that perception is governed by a moral imperative, as in the following passage:

> [Delano] . . . began indifferently pacing the poop, so as not to betray to Don Benito that he had at all mistrusted incivility, much less duplicity; for such mistrust would yet be proved illusory, and by the event. . . . [He] thought he might extremely regret it, did he allow Don Benito to become aware that he had indulged in ungenerous surmises. (65)

For Delano, only evil men fail to see the good in others, and, thus, the evil that one perceives must in reality be one's own.

---

[5] Even Delano's pervasive use of racial stereotypes, which many modern readers find offensive, would tend to have endeared readers of the mid-nineteenth century, among whom the belief in Negro inferiority was widespread. Delano is in fact typical of northern liberals and abolitionists, who commonly regarded the Negro as childlike, docile, meek, and simple (Fredrickson 97-129). In his paternal benevolence toward blacks, Delano embodies the attitude actively promoted by the romantic racialists, who took, according to Fredrickson, a "comparatively benign view of black 'peculiarities'" (101). Delano is, for instance, "invariably . . . on chatty, and half-gamesome terms" with the Negroes (84) and takes to them "not philanthropically, but genially" (84), assuming a "good humored, off-handed air" in their presence (71). Thus, behavior which the modern reader is likely to regard as condescending and objectionable was probably perceived instead by Melville's contemporaries as highly commendable in a white man. (Indeed, by no means do all modern readers even find it offensive, for at least one twentieth-century critic has judged it "plain good sense" [Cardwell 101]).

As a result, Delano's darkest suspicions all share one trait in common: their origin seems to be entirely external to him. That is, they seem to occur <u>to</u> him, rather than to emerge <u>from</u> him, as if to cast doubt on his responsibility in formulating them. It is worth noting the frequency of such phenomena:

> From no train of thought did these fancies come; <u>not from within, but from without</u>; suddenly, too, and in one throng, like hoar frost; yet as soon to vanish, as the mild sun of Captain Delano's good-nature regained its meridian. (65)

> [T]hese things now begat such return of <u>involuntary</u> suspicion, that the singular guilelessness of the American could not endure it. (67)

> Pressed by such enigmas and portents, it would have been almost against nature, had not, even into the least distrustful heart, some ugly misgivings <u>obtruded</u>. (67-68)

> [I]nsensibly he was operated on by certain general notions, which, while disconnecting pain and abashment from virtue, invariably link them with vice. (72)

> <u>From something suddenly suggested by the man's air, the mad idea now darted into Captain Delano's mind</u>, that Don Benito's plea of indisposition, in withdrawing below, was but a pretence: that he was engaged there maturing some plot. (75)

> Ah, thought he—gravely enough—this [Delano's suspicion] is like the ague: because <u>it went off</u>, it follows not that <u>it won't come back</u>. (78)

> Instantly, <u>by a fatality not to be withstood</u>, his mind, responsive to the portent, swarmed with superstitious suspicions. . . . In images far swifter than these sentences, the minutest details of <u>all his former distrusts swept through him</u>. (96; my emphasis in all of the above)

Clearly, the foregoing descriptions are designed to turn Delano into an apparently passive recipient of his "ugly misgivings" and thus to attenuate the moral dubiousness of his having entertained them. In other words, Melville creates the impression that Delano is almost too good a man even to have suspected the others of unfair play. Delano is, in fact, said to reject outright "the imputation of malign evil in man" (47), and Cereno and the tribunal confirm that "the generosity and piety of Amasa Delano [were] incapable of sounding such wickedness" (112). Thus, even though Delano turns out to be completely mistaken about the real motives of both the Spaniards and the Blacks, his fault, like that of the Greek tragic hero, is made to seem inseparable from his virtue: that is, his blindness to evil seems rooted in, and ultimately inseparable from, his very goodness.

Melville systematically reinforces the impression that Delano is good. For instance, the narrative voice continually refers to Delano as "the good seaman" (70), "good sailor" (63, 94), "good captain" (47), and "charitable man" (72), and mentions his "good nature" (47, 65, 69, 79, 96, 115) "good, blithe heart" (84), and "benevolent heart" (47). Such a constant stream of encomiums makes Delano's goodness seem somehow given or innate. Supporting testimony is offered by other characters as well. In the deposition, for instance, Delano is designated as "the generous Captain Delano" (110-111) so frequently that it becomes an epithet; he is also referred to as the "noble Captain Amasa Delano" (114) and "kind benefactor" (115). Of course, the official nature of the document seems to lend the terms credence. For his part, Delano concurs with such judgments, referring to his own "good-nature, compassion, and charity" (115) and reflecting with obvious self-satisfaction that "after good actions one's conscience is never ungrateful, however much so the benefited [sic] party may be" (97). In addition, Melville depicts Delano in characteristically charitable acts: at great personal risk and against the wary and pragmatic opposition of the mate (a detail significantly lacking from Melville's source), Delano boards an unknown ship and offers to provide it with food, water, sails, rigging, and even "three of his best seamen for temporary deck officers" to help get the ship to the nearest port (58). He himself offers to "play the pilot" (80). Delano's apparently selfless and humane response to suffering, combined with the nearly unanimous praise by distinct and apparently respectable sources around him, makes Delano's goodness seem beyond question.

The appearance of Delano's goodness and innocence is so artfully established in "BC" that Melville succeeded in hoodwinking not only his own contemporaries[6] but an astonishing number of Twentieth-Century critics as well. Among these, Leslie Fiedler is typical, who believes that "Delano fails to recognize the rebellion . . . precisely because he is a good American" (400).[7] In what follows I will seek to show that Delano's goodness and innocence are merely a mask that disguises his evil as effectively as Babo's mask of servile dedication and loyalty initially disguises the rebellion. Since goodness can be conceived only with reference to evil, it seems appropriate to begin by looking at the difference between Delano and Babo, the character most critics and readers regard as evil or, at least, as more evil than Delano.[8] Surely, if no essential moral

---

[6] Whereas critics almost universally condemned Pierre as an immoral work and even went so far as to call Melville's sanity into question, there was surprisingly very little negative criticism four years later of The Piazza Tales, in which, as William Charvat notes, Melville had indeed done "some of the darkest and bitterest writing of his life" (55). Only four reviews, all unsigned, specifically commented on "Benito Cereno." The first simply noted that the story was told "with due gravity"; the second dubbed it "a fresh specimen of Mr. Melville's sea-romances" (though not an "improvement . . . on his former popular productions in that kind"); the third found it to be "melodramatic, not effective"; and the last deemed it "most painfully interesting" (qtd. in Branch 355-59). The paucity of criticism suggests how successfully Melville had disguised his own critique of America.

[7] Other critics who judge Delano to be essentially "innocent" include Newton Arvin (240); Guy A. Cardwell (71); David D. Galloway (243); William H. Gibson (116); Allen Guttman (passim); Charles G. Hoffman (426); Harry Levin (189); R. W. B. Lewis (88); William D. Richardson (81); Michael P. Rogin (217); and Eric J. Sundquist (117). Those who see Delano as either essentially good or benevolent include R. Bruce Bickley, Jr., (102); Merlin Bowen (66); Guy A. Cardwell (72); Richard Chase (157, 158); William B. Dillingham (255); Richard H. Fogle (126); David D. Galloway (243); Edward S. Grejda (138); Tyrus Hillway (117); Sydney Kaplan (17); George Knox (281); R. W. B. Lewis (82, 88); Charles Neider (10); Barry Philips (113); Eleanor Simpson (150); Kingsley Widmer (238); and Jean Fagan Yellin (682). Other interpretations include that of Robin Magowan, who argues that Delano is a "Spenserian faerie hero" and "Knight of civilization" (348); Max Putzel, who sees Delano as "good-natured" and "optimistic" (193); William H. Shurr, who holds that Delano is "the ordinary person [who] cannot recognize the extreme of pure evil when he encounters it in 'Benito Cereno'" (154); and William Wasserstrom, for whom Delano is "the most decent and pious man on earth" (146).
Critics have only recently begun to document the hidden evil in Delano. For three especially good expositions, the reader is encouraged to see the essays by James Kavanagh, Allan Moore Emery, and Sandra Zagarell. In this essay, I will seek to add to their ground-breaking work.

[8] A partial list of critics who regard Babo as evil includes Newton Arvin (233, 240); Barbara J.

distinction obtained between the two characters, then the case for Delano's goodness would be in trouble.

Just as Melville rhetorically heightened the appearance of Delano's goodness, he also exaggerated the apparent "blackness, ten times black" (243) of Delano's "ferocious piratical" (99) antagonist Babo. Merciless killer, savage cannibal, scheming mastermind of the revolt, Babo seems a veritable devil from whose clutches only divine Providence could rescue Delano. The two characters seem to embody antithetical principles (white vs. black; free vs. slave; American vs. foreign; legitimate vs. piratical; good vs. evil), almost as if the identity of the one depended on that of the other for contrast. Nevertheless, Melville undermines all such dualities by affirming the underlying identity of the two characters: Delano and Babo are doubles.

Indeed, Delano and Babo share a systematic set of resemblances. Both, for instance, excel as commanders. Although Delano assumes that blacks are utterly incapable of command, no one fits Delano's definition of a good commander so well as Babo. Delano believes that a good commander is one who maintains "good order" (52) and who does not have "little of command but the name" (59). True to form, Babo restrains not only his own people but also his enemies, continually reminding the latter of his authority by a most effective recourse to the daily exhibition of Aranda's skeleton. Delano also believes that

---

Baines (165, 166); R. Bruce Bickley, Jr. (106-7); Merlin Bowen (203); Nicholas Canaday, Jr. (105); Guy A Cardwell (70-71); Marjorie Dew (180); Scott Donaldson (1085); Rosalie Feltenstein (247); Richard H. Fogle (138, 143-44); Bruce H. Franklin (475); David D. Galloway (242); Tyrus Hillway (118); Charles G. Hoffman (426); P. D. Johnson (433); Sydney Kaplan (20-21, 26); George Knox (281-82, 290); R. W. B. Lewis (89); James E. Miller (110); Charles Neider (10); Max Putzel (193); William D. Richardson (88); Joseph Schiffman (318); William H. Shurr (154); Eleanor Simpson (149); Arthur L. Vogelback (113-15); William Wasserstrom (145); Kingsley Widmer (65); and Stanley T. Williams (65, 74-76). My evidence for believing that most readers regard Babo as more evil than Delano is the result of years of informal sampling of my students. As a means of sparking discussion, I ask every class of mine to grade both characters on a ten-point moral scale ranging from -5 (absolute evil) to +5 (absolute good) and then to justify their grade to the rest of the class. Although individual students occasionally differ in their judgment, the classes as a whole almost invariably deem Babo more evil by at least three points. To date I have polled over 300 students.

what the San Dominick needs are "stern superior officers" (54), for the good commander knows that well-intentioned individuals are much less effective to the establishment of general quiet than "the unfriendly arm of the mate" (54). Appropriately, Babo appoints his "stern superior officers" in the form of the four oakum pickers and six hatchet polishers, who overlook the rest and keep mischief to a minimum. In addition, Delano believes in imposing perfect discipline and meeting insubordination with "instant punishment" (59). Likewise, Babo requires absolute obedience, and he is quick to punish every breach of discipline, summarily dispatching the few Spanish sailors who show the slightest sign of insubordination.

In short, Babo is an extraordinary commander. Although Delano assumes that the blacks are "too stupid" to plot anything (75), and even dismisses as incredible the idea that "every soul on board, down to the youngest negress, was [Cereno's] carefully drilled recruit in the plot" (69), Babo nearly succeeds in pulling it off. He superintends a group of unruly blacks while not appearing to do so, and he actually leads all through a hastily improvised and complex dissimulation, at the same time managing to keep a strict watch on the Spanish sailors, who are busy looking for every opportunity to alert Delano about the plot. In Babo's careful overseeing of details, in his fertile and improvised planning, in the subtle but absolute way he governs the ship to the complete bafflement of the American captain, he displays an energy and singleness of purpose that in a Spaniard or fellow American, Delano could not fail to find highly admirable.

Other parallels abound. Curiously, neither Babo nor Delano actually kills anyone in the course of the narrative, although both empower underlings to kill in their names. Thus, on Babo's command, a number of Spanish sailors are thrown overboard, and Babo personally oversees the murder of Don Alexandro by Martinqui and Lecbe. Delano likewise sends his chief mate with a boarding party to retake the San Dominick, killing nearly a score of blacks and a Spaniard in the process. Both, too, exercise tyrannical power, however they justify it to themselves. Although Babo seems "ferocious" to Delano, Delano's exercise of power is, in reality, no different. Delano may sentimentalize the social order on board his own ship as a "comfortable family of a crew" (54), but there is no question as to the nature of the "paternal" authority which must govern it: Delano merely articulates his own role when he observes of Cereno, "[N]o landsman could have dreamed that in him was lodged a dictatorship beyond which, while at sea, there was no earthly appeal" (53). Indeed, denunciations of the tyranny of sea captains form a continuous motif throughout Melville's maritime novels.

Even more tellingly, Delano and Babo are identical in their mutual enactment of the archetypal role of domination. One of Melville's most significant additions to his source is the heraldic device on the stern-piece of the San Dominick, in which there appears "a dark satyr in a mask, holding his foot on the prostrate neck of a writhing figure, likewise masked" (49). The device symbolizes the nature of political authority in the world of "BC," in which power is based on the violent subjugation of others. Babo and Delano become doubles when each by turns assumes a position of satyr-like dominance over his victim(s). Babo does this most visibly with Cereno, who is all but prostrate throughout the entire novella, and whose voice—as might be expected from the fact that the satyr's foot is on his victim's neck—is described as "hoarsely suppressed" (52). For his part, Delano, as many critics have noted, is described in terms that exactly echo those of the satyr: Delano's "foot . . . ground the prostrate negro . . . [, who] was snakishly writhing up from the boat's bottom" (99; emphasis mine). If sheer will to power is the measure, then Babo and Delano are indistinguishable from each other.

Furthermore, although Delano condemns Babo and his group as "piratical" (99), Melville suggests that Delano's claim to legitimacy is no better. Melville undermines Delano's authority by characterizing his chief mate, who leads the

American boarding party, as a former "privateer's-man" (101)—a detail absent from Melville's source. Appropriately, too, the chief mate shouts, "Follow your leader!" (102) as he boards the San Dominick—the very phrase that Babo had chalked on its prow. (Melville's allusion here to the children's game of "Follow the Leader" suggests just how ephemeral and arbitrary such authority is, as do the constant fluctuations of such characters as Babo, Atufal, and Cereno in their existential roles as master and slave.) Additionally, Melville changed the name of Delano's ship from the Perseverance to the Bachelor's Delight—the name of the ship of buccaneer William Ambrose Cowely. Finally, Melville portrayed Delano's crew as far more piratical than they appear in his source. Although Delano may be persuaded that his motive in retaking the ship is altruistic, his men certainly are motivated by no such pious sentiments: informed that the San Dominick is worth more than a thousand doubloons, of which "no small part should be theirs" (101), they respond with an enthusiastic shout which betrays their mercenary interest. Even Delano's apparently benevolent offers of assistance to Cereno in reality mask a presumptive—and piratical—preemption of power. According to Allan Moore Emery, Delano wishes to take "firm control of Cereno's vessel," and Delano is representative of Melville's confident countrymen, who would "'with pleasure' . . . have similarly taken upon themselves the responsibility for a 'spellbound' Spanish America" (53).

Although Babo and Delano double in terms of their satyr-like roles of dominance, they perhaps differ in terms of their underlying motives and in their self-understanding. Babo, for instance, seems absolutely aware of what he is doing; he indulges in no evident self-deceptions. Unlike Delano, Babo has been a slave, and he thus carries indelibly within him the knowledge of what it is like to be (in the archetypal terms of the story) the satyr's victim—knowledge that virtually overwhelms Cereno when he finally attains it. Delano, on the other hand, has never knowingly suffered as a victim; thus, he can afford the luxury of forgetfulness at the end of the novella. Moreover, Babo's ends are, as a number of critics have noted, arguably more benevolent than those of Delano. Everything that Babo does constitutes an attempt to free himself and his people. There is a grim necessity to Babo's ruthlessness; like Nat Turner he is surrounded by a hostile and technologically superior people, and he cannot succeed in his escape without the absolute coercion of the Spanish sailors under his control. This does not necessarily make his violence against others ethical (in the world of "Benito Cereno" everything is, contrarily, tinged with the greyness of moral ambiguity), but it at least helps to establish that he is no worse than Delano. Delano, on the other hand, largely acts as the agent of capitalist enterprise in retaking the ship. Although he shows a charitable respect for Spanish lives and property rights, that respect must be measured against the infinitely more heinous restoration of the blacks to slavery. In light of Melville's observation that slavery is "man's foulest crime" (Battle-Pieces, 13), Delano is clearly villainous by virtue of the sheer number of people that he in satyr-like fashion ultimately causes to be killed or returned to slavery.

Delano's complicity in slavery morally outweighs all of his other acts of kindness and charity. That is, his initially generous relief of the blacks' physical needs must be seen against his later participation in stripping them entirely of their human rights and dignity. Delano is in some ways like the southern slaveholder who prided himself on his generosity in supplying his slaves with food, shelter, and clothing even as he reduced them legally, socially, and morally to the level of beasts. Even if one were to grant that Delano's initial ignorance about blacks attenuated his guilt somewhat, such a defense could no longer hold after Delano's ignorance becomes willful. That occurs precisely when, instead of reflecting on and learning from his experience, Delano chooses to obliterate it, declaring, "[T]he past is passed; why moralize upon it? Forget it" (116). Delano's choice to forget the past is both tragic and reprehensible. To go perversely on in his blithe, sunny, self-deceived optimism even as he has newly cast the blacks into the dark night of slavery is what reveals Amasa Delano truly to be—as Melville expresses it in a characteristically bawdy pun—a masa del ano.[9]

I have argued that Melville wrote in an intentionally deceptive style. To see just how carefully restrained and insinuating Melville's style really is, all one needs to do is to compare the ending of "BC" with that of Robert Lowell's dramatized version of the novella. In Melville's "BC," Delano is left optimistically and cheerfully proposing to forget the past (and it is left entirely up to the reader to recognize how dangerous such a proposal truly is); in Lowell's "Benito Cereno," Delano murders Babo with a pistol at point-blank range. Surely both endings work; both are equally true to the sense of the work and to the character of Delano. But the subtlety is all Melville's!

Although Melville's deceptive style enabled him to publish pieces that otherwise he might not have been able to publish, and thus served to keep him afloat for the hard years after the publication of Pierre, his strategy in that regard is not the less artistic or integral to the story. "BC" is a masterpiece not only because of its innovative use of deception, but because the medium so effectively expresses the message; the story performs in effect the very deception that is its subject matter. As James Kavanagh argues,

> 'Benito Cereno' [is] a text that takes at once as its form of presentation and object of critique the peculiar preconscious mechanism—ideology—that allows one to imagine one's relation to the world in such a way as to 'feel' comfortable (i.e., fully

---

[9] Masa del ano translates literally as "mass from the anus." Although one could argue that it is simply an amazing historical coincidence, I nevertheless think it likely that Melville was aware of the irony; for he was familiar with Spanish, and he changed several other names in the novella to suit his purposes (such as "Mure" to "Babo," "Bonito Sereno" to "Benito Cereno," the Tryal to the San Dominick, etc.), but significantly left this one intact. Moreover, Melville attributes to Delano the observation that Don Benito Cereno's is "a sounding name" (64); it is hard to believe that the author was unaware of the way Amasa Delano's own name "sounds" in Spanish.

justified) about oneself, even while one is actively working to reproduce repressive social relations. . . . 'Benito Cereno' can be read as a discourse about <u>discourse,</u> about how such a mind [i. e., Delano's] <u>talks to itself,</u> giving itself the 'evidence' with which to 'perceive' and 'feel' its own useless brand of savagery as 'innocence' and 'moral simplicity.' (131)

In "BC," Melville challenges the reader to pierce through this clever rationalization of social and institutional violence and to recognize Delano's heart of darkness under his sunny and sympathetic exterior. Delano is Melville's prototypical American confidence man, one who vaunts his morality while viciously enforcing a system of black chattel slavery, who constructs a rosy future dependent on suppressing the knowledge of the past, and who refuses to accept "the imputation of malign evil in man" (47) because he can thereby remain blind to the evil in himself.

Chapter Four
The Rhetoric of the Ultra-deceptive Story

"YGB," "MRM," and "BC" share a remarkably similar structure. As we have seen, all three stories are centrally concerned with an epistemological problem about which readers are intentionally misled and about which the protagonist himself remains deluded. The question that readers must resolve in order to understand "YGB" is what actually happens to Brown in the woods; in "MRM," it is who is responsible for the L'Espanayes' death; and in "BC," it is to what extent Delano is correct in thinking the world and himself benevolent. The answers to these questions are at best implicit in the stories themselves. The masks worn by the satyr and his victim in "BC" are representative of what the reader must penetrate. In this chapter, I will examine how readers are manipulated into adopting the deluded point of view, as well as how the narratives work to free readers from it. I have for clarity's sake broken down the complex process by which point of view is corrected in these tales into three parts: 1) code-switching, or the self-conscious subversion and refiguration of the ostensible plot; 2) motivation, or the repressed psychological subtext; and 3) incrimination, or authorial value-judgment.

The ultra-deceptive story seeks at least initially to deceive the reader both by technical manipulation of the limited point of view and by appeal to a wide range of beliefs and emotions. In "YGB," for instance, the reader largely experiences events as filtered through Brown's perception; consequently, those events are likely to seem as objective and credible to the reader as they are to Brown unless and until one recognizes Brown's radical unreliability. One such instance even made so noted a critic as F. O. Mathiessen wonder whether Hawthorne was really in control of the implications of his story, so certain was Mathiessen of the literal existence of, in his words, "that damaging pink ribbon" (284) that Brown encounters in the woods. However, Mathiessen failed in this case to recognize the operative point of view, which is subtly but ironically distanced from Brown's. The narrator never actually claims that a pink ribbon fell but only that "<u>something</u> fluttered lightly down. . . . The young man seized it and <u>beheld</u> a pink ribbon" (10:83; my emphasis). In other words, the premise of the "damaging pink ribbon" is as dubious as everything else that Brown sees in the woods, since it is Brown alone who sees it. In addition, Hawthorne deliberately misleads the reader by providing false generic markers. As I argued earlier, "YGB" openly invites allegorical interpretation by the concentration of generic features that appear at the beginning as well as throughout the story. Although the allegorical mode is later subverted, many readers are already conditioned to look less skeptically upon Brown's idealization of experience.

Hawthorne also craftily seduces the reader into sharing Brown's perspective by means of the story's sexual imagery. From the ambiguously erotic sense of Brown's contemplated return to fidelity ("[A]fter this one night, I'll cling to her skirts and follow her to heaven" [10: 75]) to his symbolic penetration into the woods ("He had taken a dreary road, darkened by all the gloomiest trees of the forest, which barely stood aside to let the narrow path creep through, and closed immediately behind" [10: 75]), to his later masturbatory progress ("On he flew, among the black pines, brandishing his staff with frenzied gestures" [10: 84]), the story is fraught with sexual undertones. Such undertones, which were no doubt especially titillating for an audience accustomed to the strict taboo generally observed by Victorian writers with regard to sexual matters, tempt the reader into imaginative participation with Brown. Hawthorne's text rhetorically appeals to erotic instincts in order to increase the reader's sympathetic identification with, and pleasure in, Brown's journey.

Hawthorne similarly exploits the reader's latent voyeurism. There is, of course, a kind of pleasure in witnessing or hearing about others' sins; perhaps this is why Hawthorne's devil aptly promises his potential converts neither Faustian knowledge, nor power, nor riches, nor sensual delights, but simply the certain knowledge of sin in others:

> This night it shall be granted you to know their secret deeds . . . By the sympathy of your human hearts for sin, ye shall scent out all the places—whether in church, bedchamber, street, field, or forest—where crime has been committed, and shall exult to behold the whole earth one stain of guilt, one mighty blood spot. (10: 87)

Indeed, what reader is not strangely thrilled by the devil's revelations of secret sin in the outwardly law-abiding Puritans of Salem? Who can read the following passage without assenting at once to its essential truth and to the fact that the discovery is engrossing?

> This night it shall be granted you to know their secret deeds; how hoary-bearded elders of the church have whispered wanton words to the young maids of their households; how many a woman, eager for widows' weeds, has given her husband a drink at bedtime and let him sleep his last sleep in her bosom; how beardless youths have made haste to inherit their fathers' wealth; and how fair damsels—blush not, sweet ones!—have dug little graves in the garden, and bidden me, the sole guest, to an infant's funeral. (10: 87)

In this passage, as well as in the Devil's revelation of the sinful practices of Brown's ancestors and townsmen, Hawthorne both draws the reader into imaginative complicity with Brown and ironically depicts the Devil to a certain degree as the spokesman of truth.

To be sure, the reader is more likely than Brown to be skeptical about the claims made by the Devil (who is, after all, "the Father of lies" [John 8:44]). However, Hawthorne rhetorically heightens the Devil's credibility by presenting him as an older and wiser version of Brown—the necessary corrective, as it were, to Brown's initial and almost hopeless naiveté. Although Brown claims, for instance, "My father never went into the woods on such an errand, nor his father before him . . ." (10: 76-77), the mature reader will be more inclined to accept the devil's disclosure of the hidden sins of Brown's ancestors and townspeople because their fallibility seems humanly truer than Brown's formerly childish idealization of them as incorruptible saints. Hawthorne only catches the reader up when the trickle of individual corruption becomes an unstoppable torrent in which the whole community, even the entire human race, is implicated. If, like Brown, the reader stops short of accepting the Devil's reductio ad absurdum that evil is humanity's "only happiness" (10: 88), it is nevertheless too late for the reader to deny in any outright or innocent way that sin is indeed universal. Hawthorne has cleverly implicated the reader in the story's evil, for in imaginatively accompanying Brown into the woods and reading the devil's disclosures with voyeuristic pleasure, has not the reader also manifested "the instinct that guides mortal man to evil" [10: 83]? Nevertheless, the acknowledgment of human evil does not condemn the reader to share either the devil's views or Brown's final gloomy desperation. For one thing, Brown never admits his own evil, which for Hawthorne is the precondition for brotherhood as well as for salvation, as the tale "The Man of Adamant" amply demonstrates. Moreover, the reader need not assume that faith directly corresponds to and is evidenced by things seen, as in an allegory. Faith is rather that which must be maintained even in the face of contradictory evidence.

In "MRM," Poe created his greatest hoax. The story succeeds in deceiving readers because Dupin is so superficially impressive and because the story outwardly appeals to fantasies that virtually every reader shares. Who, after all, is not impressed by Dupin's superior intelligence and power of logical reasoning? Who can fail to admire someone who (at least apparently) solves with relative ease what no one else is capable of solving? Who, moreover, does not want to believe that the human mind can make sense of the world through the proper application of reason? Dupin seduces by the very rationality of his method, or "air of method" (17: 265), as Poe later called it. Thus, Dupin presents his ideas as a clearly reasoned and coherent argument. He recounts the thoroughgoing and methodical nature of his examination of the case and then produces what appears to be irrefutable evidence to support each inference. He limits himself rigorously to the facts. In this manner Dupin transforms himself into a compelling voice, a mesmerizing discourse emptied of all uncertainty, which sweeps everything along in its path and moves with apparently unerring precision to its goal. Even his tone when describing the path of his reasoning is emotionless, coldly intellectual, seemingly purged of human imperfection.

Poe grants Dupin, moreover, a certain rhetorical eloquence. Dupin does not state his solution directly in the manner of an amateur, but instead builds up to it slowly and suspensefully, like a masterful storyteller. He withholds information (as well as, indeed, much of the evidence) until every detail can be made to fit into his narrative—that is, until each detail is ready to be exploited for its maximum effect. Dupin even waits an entire day before informing the narrator of his purpose, so as to gain the full dramatic value of the sailor's entrance. Dupin's conclusion is meant to be stunning, and Poe seems to give his full seal of approval to it by sending the sailor in right on time, as if to verify all with an irresistible finality.

Yet, no matter how stunning his virtuosity, Dupin alone could not bamboozle the reader half so well without the help of the narrator. As readers, we may all wish we were Dupin, but it is the narrator with whom we invariably identify, and it is the narrator who both guides and articulates our response throughout the tale. As Daniel Hoffman states, "Poe tells his ratiocinative tale in such a way that the tale's author is its narrator and becomes indistinguishable from its reader. Dupin is exactly as remarkable to you and to me as he appears to his companion who tells us about his extraordinary intellectual propensities" (105). Like the laughter and the applause that are generically dubbed into many television comedies, the narrator both cues us about what to feel and validates our response. His purpose is to increase our naive admiration for—even awe of— Dupin, a role that he performs repeatedly:

> I recollected myself, and my <u>astonishment</u> was profound. "Dupin," said I, gravely, "this is <u>beyond my comprehension</u>. I do not hesitate to say that <u>I am amazed, and can scarcely credit my senses</u>. How was it possible you should know I was thinking of —
> ——?"

> . . . "Tell me, for Heaven's sake," I exclaimed, "the method—if method there is—by which you have been enabled to fathom my soul in this matter." In fact I was even more <u>startled</u> than I would have been willing to express. (4: 153)

> "—[Y]ou <u>astonish</u> me—" . . . What, then, must have been my <u>amazement</u> when I heard the Frenchman speak what he had just spoken, and when I could not help acknowledging that he had spoken the truth. (4: 154)

> I stared at the speaker in <u>mute astonishment</u>. (4: 169; my emphasis in all of the above)

The narrator heightens Dupin's intellectual prowess by serving as a foil and establishing the intellectual norm against which Dupin is to be measured. It is the narrator's own apparent inability to see that both adds suspense to the story and makes Dupin's ability seem so extraordinary. Thus, the narrator is able to praise lavishly what it would be unseemly for Dupin to praise in himself. The combination of an apparently godlike detective and ignorant but appreciative sidekick proved so effective that it was later used by the creator of Sherlock Holmes with a success that has now become legendary[1] (although Doyle seems not to have noticed how entirely deceptive was its use in "MRM").

As we saw in the preceding chapter, Melville deceives his readers by falsely heightening the appearance of Captain Delano's moral superiority. Not only does the narrator repeatedly refer to Delano as if his goodness and charity were a given, but the other Spanish characters also variously repeat and reinforce

---

[1] Doyle is lavish both in his praise and in the acknowledgment of his own debt to Poe. In <u>Memories and Adventures,</u> he writes, "Poe's masterful detective, M. Dupin, had from boyhood been one of my heroes" (69) and, in <u>Through the Magic Door</u>, "[To Poe] must be ascribed the monstrous progeny of writers on the detection of crime—'quorum pars parva fui!' Each may find some little development of his own, but his main art must trace back to those admirable stories of Monsieur Dupin. . . . Succeeding writers must necessarily be content for all time to follow in the same main track" (117-18).

this perception in the deposition that follows the retaking of the ship, lending it an air of official validation. Moreover, Melville never portrays Delano as consciously or willfully duplicitous in his dealings with others. Far from appearing in any way evil, Delano is instead depicted performing acts of charity, and he is even shown to regret his suspicions of Cereno, as if Delano were beyond entertaining evil thoughts. In fact, Melville exploits to the full the stereotype of New-World innocence in Delano, and he increases Delano's appeal to American readers by endowing the latter with representative American middle-class values, such as his work ethic, love of order, sentimentality, and liberal faith. Melville also enhances the impression of Delano's goodness by employing as a foil Babo's apparent "blackness, ten times black" (Piazza, 243), to borrow a Melvillean phrase from "Hawthorne and His Mosses." Finally, Melville cleverly manipulates the limited point of view to increase the reader's sympathy for and visceral identification with Delano as the potential victim of a dark foreign conspiracy. Although Delano's intellectual obtuseness is eventually revealed by his ignorance of the entire conspiracy, his heart has historically seemed to most readers to be in the right place, which suggests how well Melville succeeded in disguised him.

The ultra-deceptive story presents a special challenge to understanding because it assumes a generic guise that it goes on self-consciously to subvert. Interpretation is always governed to a certain extent by the reader's identification of genre, that is, by the interpretive code or set of expectations associated with the particular kind of work being read. As Alastair Fowler observes, "The generic markers that cluster at the beginning of a work have a strategic role in guiding the reader. They help to establish, as soon as possible, an appropriate mental 'set' that allows the work's generic codes to be read" (88). This mental "set" constitutes the kind of logic that will be used to relate the various elements into a coherent and intelligible whole. In The Nature of Narrative, Robert Scholes and Robert Kellogg also point to the genre-bound nature of logic when they discuss the difference between the representative (or mimetic) and illustrative (or symbolic) modes of narration. For instance, when confronted by an "empirically representative" character, we are "justified in asking questions about his motivation based on our knowledge of the ways in which real people are motivated" (87), whereas an illustrative character is referable for its meaning "not to historical, psychological, or sociological truth but to ethical and metaphysical truth" (88). Thus, the meaning of any given element in a literary work is largely a function of the pattern which governs it. In the ultra-deceptive story, the ostensible pattern is undermined by an ingeniously concealed one.

"YGB" is an excellent example. As we saw in Chapter Two, "YGB" invites allegorical interpretation by means of a cluster of generic features including the characters' universal names, the dreamlike nature of the plot, the generic guide and journey, the lack of mimetic naturalness, and the employment of idealized antithetical contrasts such as good and evil, town and forest, and day and night. However, Hawthorne strains the allegorical norm by placing it in a context of subtly mounting realism in which actuality is granted priority over ideality, a hierarchical valuation implied in the very question, "Had Goodman Brown fallen asleep in the forest and only dreamed a wild dream of a witch-meeting?" (10: 89; my emphasis). The narrator's emphasis on objective veracity is an aspect of mimetic (or representative) rather than allegorical (or illustrative) fiction. Thus, the reader is no longer authorized to interpret the ideal meaning of Brown's experience without first determining its exact empirical status. The allegorical norm is also subverted by the narrator's detached, ironic point of view, Goodman Brown's own radical unreliability, the story's suggestion of an alternative psychological explanation of events, and much more. By revealing the flaw inherent in allegorical interpretation—which ignores the resistant logic of its own vehicle—the story thereby enables the reader to transcend it in the search for a mode of interpretation that is able to do more justice to the complexity and multiplicity of human experience.

"MRM" and "BC" similarly switch codes, although in their case it is the (in Scholes' sense) mimetic code that is subverted by the symbolic one. In

"MRM," for instance, Dupin is the arch-positivist who assumes that he can intellectually control the world around him by naming and ordering its material facts. He embodies the very tendency of the detective story—which is the example of mimetic narrative par excellence—to grant ultimate significance to facts alone. As his praise of atomistic philosophy indicates, there is for Dupin no symbolic or transcendent meaning to events. Of course, every given fact means something to Dupin in the sense that, when understood correctly, it serves as an index to other facts, such as is indicated by his analysis of the narrator's thoughts based on changes in the latter's posture, or by his discovery of the physical identity of the murderer based on factual clues. However, Dupin specifically rejects illustrative or (in Scholes' sense) symbolic thinking when he affirms that there are no such things as "spirits" (4: 296), or ideal essences—the very entities that are typical of illustrative codes, as Scholes defines them. Thus, Dupin's discovery is limited to the fact that a material orangutan perpetrated the crime, a thesis that he sets forth with such seeming persuasiveness that it is no wonder that the story has been consistently misread in terms of its ostensible mimetic code. Dupin's "solution" is, however, undermined by the story's underlying symbolic code, in which the orangutan comes to have a significance undreamed of in Dupin's philosophy: rather than literally denoting the animal Pongo Pygamaeus, it metaphorically signifies an aspect of the human psyche, an essentially irrepressible libidinous force to which Dupin himself is blind. I argued in Chapter Three that Poe subtly prefigures this subversion of the story's ostensible mimetic code by redefining true analysis in the introduction as an act of the imagination, a way of seeing that grants the "spiritual" or symbolic priority over the merely literal or factual.

In "BC," Melville likewise subverts the story's ostensible mimetic code. Although in actuality a twice-told tale, "BC" seems virtually a first-hand account of historical events chosen for their peculiar dramatic interest. The story is, of course, adapted from the historical Amasa Delano's memoirs of a sea voyage, a work in a genre purporting to be strictly mimetic in Scholes' sense. Such narratives were popular in the early nineteenth century, since they sought to provide authentic accounts of both natural and anthropological wonders to which most readers lacked direct access. Melville's adaptation, much of which was lifted wholesale from his source, carefully preserves the appearance of the faithful recording of an unusual historical experience for its own sake. Indeed, the story's mimetic credentials are established as early as the opening paragraph, with its acute particularity of reference to time, place, and person:

> In the year 1799, Captain Amasa Delano, of Duxbury, in Massachusetts, commanding a large sealer and general trader, lay at anchor, with a valuable cargo, in the harbor of St. Maria—a small, desert, uninhabited island toward the southern extremity of the long coast of Chili. There he had touched for water. (46)

Such precise historical references (to be sure, Melville altered the year stated by his source, presumably to coincide with that of the slave revolt in Santo Domingo, although that alteration for artistic purposes does not affect the story's illusion of historical authenticity) are typical of the conventions of formal realism. As defined by Ian Watt in The Rise of the Novel, formal realism presents time as linear and progressive rather than as cyclic or mythical, and it depicts character as individual and historically conditioned rather than as general or archetypal (15-18, 21-25). Such conventions, which eminently exemplify the mimetic in Scholes' sense, contribute to a misleading sense of Delano's moral identity.

Delano's claim to moral superiority rests in large part on his and others' perceptions of his benevolence. One way that the conventions of formal realism serve to bolster the impression of Delano's moral goodness and innocence is by providing a privileged inside view of his intentions as such. Indeed, in post-Richardsonian fiction, human reality is increasingly constituted by psychological interiority; what characters privately think and feel defines them far more than their public identities, which are almost invariably false rhetorical masks. (One thinks, for instance, of the absolute gulf between Arthur Dimmesdale's and Hester Prynne's private and public selves.) The conventions of formal realism tend to support the view that Delano is a good man because they present Delano's benevolent intentions from the inside, as it were. The reader can seemingly verify Delano's goodness because it is clear that Delano's private intentions match his public acts; that is, one actually "overhears" him expressing the desire to help others in his thoughts. Thus, the very convention that grants the reader privileged access to Delano's thoughts seems simultaneously to confirm the reality of those thoughts.

That intentions are crucial to Delano's sense of identity is clear from his thinking, "There was a difference between the idea of Don Benito's darkly pre-ordaining Captain Delano's fate, and Captain Delano's lightly arranging Don Benito's" (70). In both cases the act (i.e., that of determining another's fate) is descriptively the same; what alone determines its morality is the motivation behind it, which, in Delano's conventional figurative usage, is either "light" or "dark"). One might say that Delano stakes his entire identity on the assumption that his own motives are "lighter," or better, than others'. However, as Alan Moore Emery has shown, Delano's seemingly benevolent offer to "play the pilot" and to "get [Benito Cereno's] ship in for him" (92) in reality masks a presumptive bid for power, in which he, as the representative of an imperialist America, wants to wrest control of the boat from the Spanish ("Manifest Destiny," 52-54). Likewise, Delano's attempt to distinguish his own intentions from those of the "ferocious" and "piratical" Babo (99) in taking over the San Dominick fails, as we saw in Chapter Four, by virtue of Melville's symbolic depiction of Delano himself as (equally) ferocious and piratical.

More broadly speaking, the impression of Delano's moral superiority rests ultimately on the perception of his mimetic difference from the other characters. The conventions of formal realism aid this perception by promoting a sense of character as historically conditioned and unique. It is, for instance, only within the mimetic code that Delano can declare of Cereno, "How unlike are we made!" (61). Superficially, Delano's statement is true: he and Cereno are from different countries; they represent different cultures; and they play different roles on board the San Dominick. The same can be said for Delano and Babo, who are even more apparently dissimilar, since they are additionally divided by race as well as by (Western vs. non-Western) heritage. However, such mimetic differences lose their relevance when seen within the story's underlying symbolic structure, in which identity is archetypally fixed. As the heraldic device of the stern-piece of the San Dominick makes clear, all identity is a function of the archetypal roles of oppressor and victim; one either dominates, like the satyr, or is dominated, like his prostrate victim. As Sandra Zagarell has argued, "No other roles [in "BC"] are structurally possible" (253). Thus, his objection notwithstanding, Delano is not in any essential way different from Cereno. Indeed, as Alan Moore Emery has shown, Delano's retaking of the San Dominick from the Spanish is an act that duplicates the earlier Spanish imperialism and in effect makes him a double of Cereno ("Manifest Destiny," 52-54). The two characters also double in being merchants, cultural types (i.e., the hearty Yankee vs. the effete Spaniard), established representatives of the social order, moral absolutists, and racists (Zagarell 249). Moreover, as we saw in Chapter Four, Delano and Babo double in their role as oppressors. There is therefore no true historical novelty or progress in the world of "BC" but only futile cyclical repetition. Given such a context, Delano's claims to moral superiority can amount to no more than a self-mystification.

In the ultra-deceptive short story, semiotic code-switching has the effect not only of undermining each protagonist's world view, but also of recasting the plot entirely along a different set of narrative vectors, thus essentially altering the dynamic relationships that obtain between the various narrative elements within the story. In other words, the ostensibly objective order of events is supplanted by a latent subjective one, whose hidden mechanism of distortion forms the real vector of plot. One practical result of discovering this latent source of causality is that more narrative elements are unified and made cohesive by the new sense of the whole that obtains, while many elements which may have been previously "disturbing" are also explained.[2]

In "YGB," for instance, all of the seemingly objective events in the woods are seen to be subjectively motivated by the desires of Brown, who seeks to free himself of guilt by stifling his potential critics and implicating the entire town in his own contemplated misdeeds. Thus, as we saw in Chapter Two, it is Brown who determines the identity and order of appearance of the other characters in the woods. The discovery that Brown is projecting his own desires onto others makes manifest the latent causality of plot, in which narrative elements that otherwise seem merely coincidental obtain a new logic and cohesiveness. It helps to explain, for instance, why the Devil looks like an older and wiser version of Brown, why Martha Carrier is described in the exact words of Cotton Mather, and why so much of the devil's mass occurs within a transformed natural context, to name just a few. The recognition of a psychological subtext renders significant other features of the narrative as well, such as the consistent ironic distance between the narrator and Brown and the final display of loyalty by a community that Brown had deemed utterly evil.

"MRM" is likewise governed by a latent psychological causality. The severance of Madam L'Espanaye's head from her body dramatically represents the larger conflict between head and body that operates within the narrative, a conflict evinced both by the symbolic doubling of the characters as aspects of a head/body dichotomy and by Dupin's own schizophrenic repression of emotion. This repression—most notable in Dupin's pathologically emotionless manner while thinking, as well as in his inability to feel anything at all toward the objects of his analysis—is what symbolically gives rise to the orangutan, the volcanic

---

[2] Sigurd Burckhardt uses the term "disturbing" in his theory of intrinsic interpretation to describe an element which produces a discrepancy between one's conception of a work of art and the work of art itself. He states, "[interpretation] begins when I recognize that this conception is an initial and possibly subconscious hypothesis, which must be revised in accordance with the text. . . . The revision of one's hypothesis must proceed in such a way that the disturbing element is finally proved both reasonable and necessary—.e., the new hypothesis must account for the previously disturbing element" (302).

force of long-repressed libido that is responsible for the dismemberment of Dupin's double, Madam L'Espanaye.

It is significant that no moral responsibility for the murders exists until the story's plot is conceived of in symbolic terms. The idea of moral responsibility is conspicuously absent from Dupin's own objective reconstruction of the circumstances leading up to the L'Espanayes' death. By denying the idea of a motive, Dupin effectively precludes the possibility of a morally significant cause altogether. Thus the discrepancy between the two versions of what happens to the L'Espanayes constitutes far more than just a disagreement over "whodunit"; it entails a much greater disparity over the very nature and meaning of the event itself and even, in some ways, of the universe in which it occurs. If, for instance, the essential function of the detective is, as Peter Brooks suggests in Reading for the Plot, to reconstruct the plot (23-29), then it is remarkable that the plot which Dupin constructs contains neither a crime, nor even an element of tragedy, but merely an accident—a chance occurrence. Crime and responsibility need not, of course, be ingredients of every good detective story, but in a story that defines analysis as a "moral activity which disentangles" (4: 146; first emphasis mine), analysis should presumably be concerned with disentangling questions of moral responsibility rather than meaningless puzzles.

Dupin's reconstruction also fails to explain many elements of the narrative that a recognition of psychological causality renders significant. These include the similarity in the living arrangements of, respectively, the L'Espanayes and the narrator and Dupin, as well as the many suggestions of mental illness within the story. The latter include the references to Dupin's "diseased intelligence" (4: 152) and to themselves as "madmen" (4: 151) who inhabit an old mansion that is "tottering to its fall" (4: 151). Thus, it is only when the events of the story are seen in their ideal or metaphorical light—as, by identifying true analysis with the imagination, Poe's introduction both authorizes and requires us to do—that the real human significance of the tale becomes apparent. In this manner, Poe asserts not only the superiority of symbolic over mimetic fiction (or, as he puts it, the "suggestive" and "spiritual" [10: 65] over the purely literal and factual), but also, and especially, the priority of spirit over matter, which Poe so often depicted in his fiction.

A psychological structure likewise governs "BC," in which Delano's benevolence is revealed to be the subterfuge of a self-deceived mind. Everything that Delano sees is, in fact, transformed by unconscious desires; like Young Goodman Brown, he perceives nothing without implicitly bestowing upon it a valuation which it lacks in reality. Not only does he misread the plot on board the San Dominick, but he ultimately misconstrues even his own intentions. He does this because he is driven by the obsession to legitimate the exercise of his own will to power. He simply cannot enslave so many people in satyr-like fashion without masking both to himself and others his true motives. Thus Delano comes to assert hierarchical moral differences where the narrative demonstrates only symbolic moral equivalencies, and his paternalism and charity serve merely to disguise the nature of his participation in, and perpetuation of, oppressive social, political, and economic institutions. The revelation of Delano's secret "plot" for dominance constitutes the real plot of "BC."

The ultra-deceptive story rhetorically condemns the ideology of its protagonist by directly implicating him in an act or acts of criminal violence within the narrative. This violence is shown to arise directly from the character's ideology itself, which cannot be understood apart from its effects. The trope of criminality provides a means of intratextual evaluation. It is a topos, or common ground, upon which the writer and reader can agree about questions of value. Readers may, for instance, disagree widely about the meaning of a work such as King Lear, but virtually no one would disagree that it is wrong for Cornwall to gouge out Gloucester's eyes or for Edmond to order Cordelia killed. Indeed, Shakespeare employs such obvious transgressions precisely to shape his audience's response toward the characters that perform them. So, too, in the ultra-deceptive story, the protagonist's association with criminal violence of some sort exposes the fundamental inhumanity of his views.

In "YGB," the protagonist is clearly implicated in the notorious Salem witch trials by virtue of the tale's many allusions to them. Brown shares, for instance, the theological beliefs which provided the framework and justification for the trials, and his identification of Martha Carrier in the words of Cotton Mather (10: 86) serves to associate him with the eminent Puritan theologian who influenced the outcome of the hangings. Moreover, Brown judges his fellow townsmen on the grounds of the same kind of specter evidence that was credited at the trials, and he himself exhibits the same morally dubious motives as those who made the historical accusations. Although the reader only views Faith through his point of view, one may surmise that for her this newly "stern," "sad," "darkly meditative," "distrustful, if not . . . desperate" husband who "shrank from [her] bosom," "scowled, and muttered to himself, and gazed sternly at his wife, and turned away" (10: 89) would not be the easiest man to live with.

In "MRM," the crime is clearly calculated to impress the reader: in Dupin's words,

> On the hearth were thick tresses—very thick tresses—of grey human hair. These had been torn out by the roots. . . . Their roots (a hideous sight!) were clotted with fragments of the flesh of the scalp—sure token of the prodigious power which had been exerted in uprooting perhaps half a million of hairs at a time. The throat of the old lady was not merely cut, but the head absolutely severed from the body: the instrument was a mere razor. I wish you also to look at the brutal ferocity of these deeds. Of the bruises upon the body of Madame L'Espanaye I do not speak. . . . (4: 180)

The description is, in fact, so graphic and shocking that one wonders how anyone could treat the whole thing as casually as Dupin does when he suggests that an examination into the particulars of the crime "will afford [himself and the narrator] amusement" (4: 167). As we saw in Chapter 2, Dupin's intellectual control and aloofness is itself symbolically implicated in the crime. In living on the fourth floor (the equivalent of the mind in the house-as-body metaphor) and repressing normal (i.e., for Poe, heterosexual) behavior, Dupin and the narrator are doubles of the L'Espanayes, who represent similar emotional repression. Such repression is an aspect of the head's domination of the body, in token of which Madame L'Espanaye's head is ultimately severed from her body. The body's resistance to emotional repression is symbolized, in turn, by a third set of doubles, the sailor in port and the orangutan, who themselves—one by proverb and the other by proxy—embody the liberation of libido in the form of unrestrained sexual activity, a force so powerful that it virtually blows the L'Espanayes apart. Dupin's failure to achieve integration of his intellect and emotions is suggested by his alternating use of two incompatible voices—which doubles the two voices (one clearly intelligible and the other lacking syllabification) of the sailor and the orangutan. In short, it is precisely Dupin's inordinate intellectual propensity that symbolically creates the necessary conditions of, and is thus responsible for, the murders.

The crimes in "BC" are all symbolized by the archetypal image of the masked satyr violently dominating his victim. The satyr is depicted "holding his foot on the prostrate neck of a writhing figure, likewise masked" (49)—the very position that Delano assumes in the boat with Babo (99). The masks worn by the satyr and his victim symbolize the equivocation of perception; just as the victim is masked, so Delano remains unaware of Cereno's real condition throughout the latter's entire ordeal on the San Dominick, as well as of the condition of oppressed blacks in general. Moreover, just as the satyr is masked, so Delano masks his own identity as oppressor from everyone, including himself. The victims cannot, however, indulge in such cheerful obliviousness, for they are brought to a full and agonized consciousness of their subjugated status, as Benito's vivid terror at the sight of Babo's razor makes clear. In fact, the awareness of what it is like to be a victim is so forcible that Benito cannot forget it even after the ordeal is over, despite Delano's remonstrations. Benito's consciousness of victimization speaks eloquently for all of the victims in "Benito Cereno" and thus ironically functions as a condemnation of the man who, by restoring slavery to the San Dominick and "gr[inding] the prostrate negro" (99), ultimately victimizes the greatest number of people.

We have seen that the ultra-deceptive story works by willful indirection. It lures readers into adopting the point of view of a self-deluded and criminal protagonist, and the correction that it offers is at best implicit, dependent upon the reader's recognition that a different literary code is operative within the story. The ultra-deceptive story thus presents the reader with a moral test of sorts. Although it lacks explicit authorial commentary, it nevertheless conveys a moral judgment and, in fact, implicitly prejudges the reader's response. Of course, readers are not entirely constrained by such a judgment. In the dialectical confrontation of values that constitutes reading at its best, the reader may, in turn, deem the text's judgment rhetorically heavy-handed, oversimplified, or in some other manner inadequate. However, the reader who ignores such judgment not only misses the point of the story, but also runs the risk that the text's fabular warning of the dangers of ideological blindness in interpretation may, after all, prove prophetic. Moreover, the reader who ignores such judgment likewise forfeits the opportunity that the ultra-deceptive story presents for moral growth. By dramatizing both the violence inherent in our common ways of seeing and the strategies by which we ideologically mask this violence to ourselves, the ultra-deceptive story reveals the potential criminal in all of us and thereby exhorts us to an unceasing examination of our critical habits of mind. This is at once the brilliance and the burden of its rhetorical deception.

Bibliography

Adams, Henry. The Education of Henry Adams. Boston and New York: Houghton Mifflin, 1918.

Adler, Joyce Sparer. War in Melville's Imagination. New York: New York UP, 1981.

"Allegory." The Concise Oxford Dictionary of Literary Terms. 1990.

"Allegory." A Dictionary of Modern Critical Terms. Rev. ed. 1987.

Arvin, Newton. Herman Melville. Sloane, 1950.

Austen, Jane. Emma. Ed. Lionel Trilling. Boston: Houghton Mifflin, 1957.

Baines, Barbara J. "Ritualized Cannibalism in 'Benito Cereno.'" ESQ: A Journal of the American Renaissance 30.3 (1984): 163-69.

Bell, Michael D. Hawthorne and the Romance of New England. Princeton, N. J.: Princeton UP, 1971.

Bickley, R. Bruce, Jr. The Method of Melville's Short Fiction. Durham, N. C.: Duke UP, 1975.

Bloom, Edward A. "The Allegorical Principle." ELH 18 (1951): 163-90.

Booth, Wayne. The Rhetoric of Fiction. 1961. Chicago: U of Chicago P, 1983.

——. A Rhetoric of Irony. Chicago: U of Chicago P, 1974.

Bowen, Merlin. The Long Encounter: Self and Experience in the Writings of Herman Melville. Chicago: U of Chicago P, 1960.

Branch, Watson G. Melville: The Critical Heritage. Boston, Mass.: Routledge and Kegan Paul, 1974.

Burckhardt, Sigurd. Shakespearean Meanings. Princeton, N.J.: Princeton UP, 1968.

Burr, George Lincoln, ed. Narratives of the Witchcraft Cases, 1648-1706. New

York: C. Scribner's Sons, 1914.

Canaday, Nicholas, Jr. "A New Reading of Melville's 'Benito Cereno.'" Studies in American Literature. Eds. Waldo McNeir and Leo B. Levy. Baton Rouge: Louisiana State UP, 1960.

Cardwell, Guy. "Melville's Gray Story: Symbols and Meaning in 'Benito Cereno.'" Bucknell Review 8 (1959): 154-67. Rpt. Herman Melville: Modern Critical Views. Ed. Harold Bloom. New York, New Haven, and Philadelphia: Chelsea, 1986.

Charvat, William. "Melville and the Common Reader." Studies in Bibliography 12 (1959): 41-57.

Chase, Richard. Herman Melville: A Critical Study. New York: Macmillan, 1949.

Colacurcio, Michael J. The Province of Piety. Cambridge, Mass.: Harvard UP, 1984.

Coleridge, Samuel Taylor. Biographia Literaria. Ed. J. Shawcross. London: Oxford UP, 1973.

Crews, Frederick C. The Sins of the Fathers: Hawthorne's Psychological Themes. New York: Oxford UP, 1966.

Cuvier, Baron. The Animal Kingdom. Trans. W. B. Carpenter and J. O. Westwood. New York: Kraus Reprint, 1969.

Defoe, Daniel. Selected Writings of Daniel Defoe. Ed. James T. Boulton. New York: Cambridge UP, 1975.

Delano, Amasa. Narrative of Voyages. Boston, 1817.

Dew, Marjorie. "'Benito Cereno': Melville's Vision and Revision of the Source," A "Benito Cereno" Handbook. Belmont, Cal.: Wadsworth, 1965.

Dillingham, William B. Melville's Short Fiction 1853-56. Athens, Ga.: U of Georgia P, 1977.

Donaldson, Scott. "The Dark Truth of the Piazza Tales." PMLA 85 (1970): 1082-86.

Doyle, Sir Arthur Conan. Memories and Adventures. Boston: Little, Brown, 1924.

——. Through the Magic Door. New York: McClure, 1908.

Emery, Alan Moore. "'Benito Cereno' and Manifest Destiny." Nineteenth-Century Fiction 39 (1984): 48-68.

——. "The Topicality of Depravity in 'Benito Cereno.'" American Literature 55 (1983): 316-31

"Epicurus." The Encyclopedia of Philosophy. 1967 ed.

Engell, James. The Creative Imagination: Enlightenment to Romanticism. Cambridge, Mass.: Harvard UP, 1981.

Feltenstein, Rosalie. "'Benito Cereno': from Source to Symbol." A "Benito Cereno" Handbook. Belmont, Cal.: Wadsworth, 1965.

Fiedler, Leslie A. Love and Death in the American Novel. New York: Stein and Day, 1975.

Fogle, Richard H. Melville's Shorter Tales. Norman, Ok.: U of Oklahoma P, 1960.

Forster, E. M. Aspects of the Novel. 1927. New York: Harcourt, Brace: 1956.

Fletcher, Angus. Allegory: The Theory of a Symbolic Mode. Ithaca, New York: Cornell UP, 1964.

Fowler, Alastair. Kinds of Literature: An Introduction to the Theory of Genres and Modes. Cambridge, Mass.: Harvard UP, 1982.

Franklin, Bruce H. "'Apparent Symbol of Despotic Command': Melville's 'Benito Cereno.'" New England Quarterly 34 (1961): 462-77.

Fredrickson, George M. The Black Image in the White Mind. New York: Harper and Row, 1971.

Galloway, David D. "Herman Melville's 'Benito Cereno': An Anatomy." Texas Studies in Literature and Language 9 (1967): 239-52.

Gibson, William H. "Herman Melville's 'Bartleby the Scrivener' and 'Benito Cereno.'" The History of an Era: Essays and Interpretations. Ed. George Hendrick. Frankfurt: Diesterweg, 1961.

Grejda, Edward S. The Common Continent of Men: Racial Equality in the Writings of Herman Melville. Port Washington, N. Y.: Kennikat, 1974.

Guttman, Allen. "The Enduring Innocence of Captain Amasa Delano." Boston University Studies in English 5 (1961): 35-46.

Hankins, Thomas L. Science and the Enlightenment. New York: Cambridge UP, 1985.

Hawthorne, Nathaniel. The Centenary Edition of the Works of Nathaniel Hawthorne. 13 vols. Eds. William Charvat, Roy H. Pearce and Claude M. Simpson. Ohio State UP, 1974.

Haycraft, Howard. Murder for Pleasure: The Life and Times of the Detective Story. New York: D. Appleton-Century, 1941.

Henry, O. The Best Short Stories of O. Henry. Eds. Bennett A. Cerf and Van H. Cartmell. New York: Modern Library, 1945.

Hillway, Tyrus. Herman Melville. New York: Twayne, 1963.

Hoffman, Daniel. Poe Poe Poe Poe Poe Poe Poe. Garden City, N.Y.: Doubleday, 1972.

Hoffman, Charles G. "The Shorter Fiction of Herman Melville." The South Atlantic Quarterly 52 (1953): 414-30.

Honig, Edwin. Dark Conceit. New York: Oxford UP, 1959.

Hostetler, Norman H. "Narrative Structure and Theme in 'Young Goodman Brown.'" The Journal of Narrative Technique 12 (1982 Fall): 221-28.

Howard, Leon. Herman Melville. Berkeley and Los Angeles, Calif.: U of California P, 1958.

——. "Historical Note." Pierre. Eds. Harrison Hayford, Hershel Parker, and G. Thomas Tanselle. Evanston and Chicago: Northwestern UP and The Newberry Library, 1971.

Humma, John B. "'Young Goodman Brown' and the Failure of Hawthorne's Ambiguity." Colby Library Journal 9 (1971): 425-31.

Hurley, Paul J. "Young Goodman Brown's 'Heart of Darkness.'" New England Quarterly 37 (1966): 410-19.

Iser, Wolfgang. The Implied Reader: Patterns of Communication in Prose Fiction from Bunyan to Beckett. Baltimore and London: The Johns Hopkins UP, 1974.

James, Henry. Hawthorne 1879. Ithaca, N. Y.: Cornell UP, 1967.

Johnson, P. D. "American Innocence and Guilt: Black-White Destiny in 'Benito Cereno.'" Phylon 36 (1975): 426-34.

Joyce, James. A Portrait of the Artist as a Young Man. 1916. New York: Penguin, 1984.

Kaplan, Sydney. "Herman Melville and the American National Sin: The Meaning of 'Benito Cereno.'" Journal of Negro History 42 (1957): 11-37.

Kavanagh, James H. "'That Hive of Subtlety': 'Benito Cereno' as Critique of Ideology." Bucknell Review: The Arts, Society, Literature. Ed. Harry R. Garvin. Lewisburg: Bucknell UP, 1984. 127-57.

Ketterer, David. Poe and the Rationale of Deception. Baton Rouge: Louisiana State UP, 1979.

Knox, George. "Lost Command: 'Benito Cereno' Reconsidered." The Personalist 40.3 (1959): 280-91.

De Lacy, P. H. "Epicurus." The Encyclopedia of Philosophy. 1967.

Lathrop, George P. A Study of Hawthorne. Boston: J. R. Osgood, 1876.

Lawrence, D. H. Studies in Classic American Literature. 1923. New York:

Viking, 1973.

Lemay, Leo B. "The Psychology of the 'Murders in the Rue Morgue.'" <u>American Literature</u> 54 (1982): 165-88.

Levin, David. "Shadows of Doubt: Specter Evidence in Hawthorne's 'Young Goodman Brown.'" <u>American Literature</u> 34 (1962): 344-52.

Lewis, C. S. <u>The Allegory of Love</u>. Oxford: Oxford UP, 1936.

Levin, Harry. <u>The Power of Blackness: Hawthorne, Poe, Melville</u>. New York: Knopf, 1958.

Levy, Leo B. "The Problem of Faith in 'Young Goodman Brown.'" <u>Journal of English and Germanic Philology</u> 74 (1975): 375-87.

Lewis, R. W. B. "Melville After <u>Moby Dick</u>: The Tales." <u>Herman Melville: Modern Critical Views</u>. Ed. Harold Bloom. New York, New Haven, and Philadelphia: Chelsea, 1986. 77-90.

Liebman, Sheldon W. "The Reader in 'Young Goodman Brown.'" <u>Nathaniel Hawthorne Journal</u> 5 (1975): 156-69.

Lowell, Robert. "Benito Cereno." <u>The Old Glory</u>. New York: Farrar, Straus, and Giroux, 1965. 115-194.

Lowndes, Robert A. W. "The Contributions of Edgar Allan Poe." <u>The Mystery Writer's Art</u>. Ed. Francis M. Nevins, Jr. Bowling Green: Bowling Green University Popular Press, 1970. 1-15.

Magowan, Robin. "Masque and Symbol in Melville's 'Benito Çereno.'" <u>College English</u> 23 (1962): 346-51.

Martin, Terence. <u>Nathaniel Hawthorne</u>. Revised ed. Boston: Twayne Publishers, 1983.

Mathiessen, F. O. <u>American Renaissance</u>. New York: Oxford UP, 1966.

Maupassant, Guy de. <u>Selected Stories</u>. Trans. and ed. Dora Knowlton Ranous. vol. 1. New York: Leslie-Judge, 1912.

May, Charles E. "The Nature of Knowledge in Short Fiction." <u>The New Short Story Theories</u>. Ed. Charles E. May. Athens, Ohio: Ohio UP, 1994.

McKeithan, D. M. "Hawthorne's 'Young Goodman Brown': An Interpretation." <u>Modern Language Notes</u> 67 (1952): 93-96.

Melville, Herman. <u>Battle-Pieces and Aspects of the War: Civil War Poems</u>. Edited and with an Introduction by Lee Rust Brown. New York: Da Capo, 1995.

——. <u>Correspondence</u>, vol. 14 of <u>The Writings of Herman Melville</u>, edited by Lynne Horth. Evanston, Ill.: Northwestern UP and Newberry Library, 1993.

——. Moby-Dick or The Whale, vol. 6 of The Writings of Herman Melville, edited by Harrison Hayford, Hershel Parker, and G. Thomas Tanselle. Evanston, Ill.: Northwestern UP and Newberry Library, 1988.

——. The Piazza Tales and Other Prose Pieces, 1839-1860, vol. 9 of The Writings of Herman Melville, edited by Harrison Hayford, Hershel Parker, and G. Thomas Tanselle. Evanston, Ill.: Northwestern UP and Newberry Library, 1987.

Miller, James E. A Reader's Guide to Herman Melville. New York: Octagon, 1963.

Miller, Paul W. "Hawthorne's 'Young Goodman Brown': Cynicism or Meliorism?" Nineteenth-Century Fiction 14 (1959): 260.

Mortimer, Armine Kotin. "Second Stories." Short Story Theory at a Crossroads. Eds. Susan Lohafer and Jo Ellyn Clarey. Baton Rouge and London: Louisiana State UP, 1989. 276-98.

Mosher, Jr. Harold F. "The Source of Ambiguity in Hawthorne's 'Young Goodman Brown.'" ESQ: A Journal of the American Renaissance 26 (1980): 16-25.

Neider, Charles. Introduction. Short Novels of the Masters. New York: Rinehart, 1948.

O. Henry. The Best Short Stories of O. Henry. Selected and with an Introduction by Bennett A. Cerf and Van H. Cartmell. New York: Modern Library, 1945.

Parker, Hershel. "Why Pierre Went Wrong." Studies in the Novel 8 (1976): 7-23.

——, and Higgins, Brian. "The Flawed Grandeur of Melville's Pierre." New Perspectives on Melville. Ed. Faith Pullin. Edinburgh: Edinburgh UP, 1978. 162-96.

Phillips, Barry. "'The Good Captain': Amasa Delano, American Idealist." A "Benito Cereno" Handbook. Belmont, Calif.: Wadsworth, 1965.

Poe, Edgar Allen. The Complete Works of Edgar Allan Poe. 17 vols. Ed. James A. Harrison. New York: AMS Press, 1965.

Putzel, Max. "The Source and the Symbols of Melville's 'Benito Cereno.'" American Literature 34 (1962): 191-206.

Richardson, William D. Melville's "Benito Cereno": An Interpretation with Annotated Text and Concordance. Durham, N. C.: Carolina Academic Press, 1987.

Rogin, Michael P. Subversive Genealogy: The Politics and Art of Herman Melville. New York: Knopf, 1983.

Rohrberger, Mary. Hawthorne and the Modern Short Story. The Hague & Paris:

Mouton, 1966.

Schiffman, Joseph. "Critical Problems in Melville's 'Benito Cereno.'" Modern Language Quarterly 11 (1950): 317-24.

Shurr, William H. The Mystery of Iniquity. Lexington, Ken.: UP of Kentucky, 1972.

Simpson, Eleanor. "Melville and the Negro: From 'Typee' to 'Benito Cereno.'" On Melville: The Best from American Literature. Eds. Louis J. Budd and Edwin Cady. Durham, N. C.: Duke UP, 1988.

Stearns, Frank Preston. The Life and Genius of Nathaniel Hawthorne. Philadelphia and London: J. B. Lippincott, 1906.

Stewart, Randall. Nathaniel Hawthorne: A Biography. New Haven: Yale UP, 1948.

Stovall, Floyd. Edgar Poe the Poet. Charlottesville: Virginia UP, l969.

Sundquist, Eric J. "Suspense and Tautology in 'Benito Cereno.'" Glyph: Textual Studies 8 (Baltimore: Johns Hopkins UP, 1981). 103-26.

Sutherland, James. Daniel Defoe: A Critical Study. Cambridge, Mass.: Harvard UP, 1971.

Swift, Jonathan. Gulliver's Travels and Other Writings. Ed. Ricardo Quintana. New York: Modern Library, 1958.

Vogelback, Arthur L. "Shakespeare and Melville's 'Benito Cereno.'" Modern Language Notes 67 (1952): 113-16.

Wasserstrom, William. "Melville the Mannerist: Form in the Short Fiction." Herman Melville: Reassessments. Ed. A. Robert Lee. Totowa, N. J.: Barnes & Noble, 1984.

Widmer, Kingsley. "The Perplexity of Melville: 'Benito Cereno.'" Studies in Short Fiction 5 (Spring 1968): 225-238.

——. The Ways of Nihilism: A Study of Herman Melville's Short Novels. Los Angeles, Calif.: California State Colleges, 1970.

Williams, Stanley T. "'Follow Your Leader': Melville's 'Benito Cereno.'" Virginia Quarterly Review 23 (1947): 61-76.

Wright, Austin. "On Defining the Short Story: The Genre Question." Short Story Theory at a Crossroads. Eds. Susan Lohafer and Jo Ellyn Clarey. Baton Rouge and London: Louisiana State UP, 1989. 46-53.

Yellin, Jean Fagan. "Black Masks: Melville's 'Benito Cereno.'" American Quarterly 22 (1970): 678-89.

Zagarell, Sandra A. "Reenvisioning America: Melville's 'Benito Cereno.'" ESQ: A Journal of the American Renaissance 30 (1984): 245-59.

Index

100

STUDIES IN COMPARATIVE LITERATURE